*Why Feel Guilty
About Feeling Good?*

The

Joy of
Self-
Pleasuring

Edward L. Rowan, M.D.

Prometheus Books

59 John Glenn Drive
Amherst, New York 14228-2197

Published 2000 by Prometheus Books

Inquiries should be addressed to
Prometheus Books
59 John Glenn Drive
Amherst, New York 14228–2197
VOICE: 716–691–0133, ext. 207
FAX: 716–564–2711
WWW.PROMETHEUSBOOKS.COM

04 03 02 01 00   5 4 3 2 1

Library of Congress Cataloging-in-Publication Data

Rowan, Edward L.
    The joy of self-pleasuring : why feel guilty about feeling good? /
Edward L. Rowan.
        p.   cm.
    Includes bibliographical references.
    ISBN 1–57392–995–3 (pbk. : alk. paper)
    1. Masturbation. I. Title.

HQ447 .R68 2000
306.77'2—dc21   99–059071
                                                       CIP

Printed in the United States of America on acid-free paper

Contents

Acknowledgments

When I first started talking about this topic, someone said, "A book about masturbation? I would think a paragraph or two would do." Now, many paragraphs—and years—later, the task is accomplished. It is not "done," as there is always much more to learn and share.

In the course of my journey with this book, many people have helped. Thanks first to the patients who shared their stories, then to Phil Roberts in New Zealand, Dr. John Price in England, Dr. John Money in Baltimore, the late Dr. Bill Hartman in San Diego, and Dr. Vern Bullough in Los Angeles. Their support and encouragement at exactly the right moments was critical. Library staff at Concord Hospital, Porirua Hospital, St. Anselm's College, Dartmouth Medical School, and the University of New Hampshire were very helpful. Special thanks to Chris Cunnar at the Human Relations Area Files for her assistance. Steven Mitchell and Meg French at Prometheus did a superb editing job and caused me to think hard about what I was saying.

Especially, I thank Judy for her love, her support, her ideas and suggestions, but mostly for accepting the role as "the wife of the man who wrote the book about masturbation."

Introduction

The year 1994 was particularly bad for masturbation. On December 12, President Bill Clinton fired the surgeon general. Dr. Joycelyn Elders had said something "controversial" when she supported "some explicit discussion and promotion of masturbation" in schools as one way to limit the spread of HIV and AIDS. Especially since masturbation is ideal preventive medicine for unwanted pregnancy and sexually transmitted diseases, it's hard to understand the reason behind the sacking.

Government officials always seem to be saying controversial things. Statements about abortion, gay rights, smoking and cancer, school prayer, gun control, animal lab testing, battery hen farming, nuclear power plants, euthanasia, whaling, spotted owls, a balanced budget, evolution, or the United Nations will mobilize groups on both sides of the issue. They will march, carry signs, and say even more controversial things about each other. So, controversy, per se, must not be the reason.

Masturbation is a common activity with which all of us are familiar. Well, almost all of us. A couple of ultraconservative senators must have had mothers who sewed up the flaps in their Dr. Dentons and taught them the hands-off policy toward "down there." The rest of us had a grip on the situation. So masturbation, per se, must not be the reason.

The fight against AIDS requires all the weapons and strategies that we can muster. Given the choice of a glory hole or any other form of unprotected sex versus masturbation, there is no question as to which orgasm is safest. The Clinton administration has found money for research into drugs for AIDS and for promoting safe sex. The previous surgeon general, C. Everett Koop, had even suggested that condom use could reduce the spread of sexually transmitted diseases. So AIDS prevention must not be the reason.

Tune into any daytime talk show and hear seemingly ordinary people talk about really weird sexual stuff. Talking about sexually explicit material must not be the reason.

Administration officials said that Elders's statement was at odds with administration policy and that she had been previously warned to "be more discreet." There are those who believe that some administration policy is equivalent to jerking off; however, the surgeon general was apparently seen as too liberal and the administration was trying to shift to the Right after a disastrous election. The president was looking for an excuse to fire her and Dr. Elders finally made a comment about a cause without a lobby. No one came forth to announce that they would withhold votes or money if they couldn't masturbate. No one marched around the White House with signs like "Up with Wankers," "Free Your Willy," "Jill-Off Power," or "Honk If You Do Solo Sex." There was no write-in campaign to bring back the lady who told the truth. The administration finally found an issue that tapped into the collective shame and guilt of the population. There was no major movement to go public in support of masturbation. There was no public opposition to firing Dr. Elders.

Nineteen ninety-four also saw the publication of two major books about sexual behavior. One looked at the United States and the other looked at Britain. The British book doesn't mention masturbation at all. It's not that the Brits don't wank their willies or polish their pearls. They do. A pretest found the subject of masturbation "distasteful and embarrassing." The authors didn't want to prejudice the rest of their study by asking about something distasteful, so they left it out.[1] In the United States, it was handled differently. A pretest found the subject "uncomfortable," so four questions about masturbation were asked on self-response forms and put in sealed envelopes before being handed to inter-viewers.[2] We'll look at these studies later, but the point is that it is extremely difficult to ask people about their mas-turbatory habits. They would rather tell a stranger their annual salary than how many times they have masturbated in the last week. They would be ashamed and feel guilty and they won't talk about jerking off.

Nineteen ninety-six should have been a better year. *Sperm Wars* was published in the United States. It was first published in England in 1994 as *Human Sperm Competition*. That says something about cultural differences, but that's another story. *Sperm Wars* argues persuasively that mastur-bation is a "natural activity" from the perspective of evolu-tionary biology. Masturbation is critical to survival of the fittest because it keeps the youngest, most active sperm at the head of the column to be ejaculated and in the best posi-tion to fertilize an available egg. In order to maintain his competitive advantage, a man must keep other men from masturbating while continuing to do so himself, explaining the paradox of universal condemnation of a universal prac-tice.[3] This was a real intellectual breakthrough, but it seems to have gone completely unnoticed. Sometimes, I think I bought the only copy of the book sold in the United States.

Shame and guilt rule. We are mired in a view of "natural

activity" formulated at a time when it was "natural" for the sun to revolve around a flat earth, sperm was equated with vegetable seed, and sexual fulfillment for a woman required the presence of a man. Science has come a long way since then, but elements of society have yet to catch up.

As a psychiatrist and sex therapist, I dealt with that shame and guilt professionally for thirty years, starting long before 1994. It's a problem when, by a sense of entitlement or shame, a man will force sex on a partner—or even a stranger—rather than use his hand. It's a problem when a man having difficulty in sexual performance won't rehearse a better behavior pattern or accept the need to masturbate. It's a problem when a woman cannot use masturbation to learn how to have a pleasurable sexual experience.

As a man, I've been dealing with the shame and guilt of masturbation personally since I was a kid. Most of us have. It's part of the socialization process.

The effects of masturbation on sexual development really became clear to me about fifteen years ago, when I started working with sex offenders. As part of the development of a treatment program within a correctional setting, I reviewed many sex education curricula. Many authors have quoted from old Scout handbooks when they wanted a really bad example of teaching about sexuality. I reviewed the handbooks myself, and also wrote a paper about it.[4] The Scouts have always avoided the topic of masturbation. Now, don't get me wrong: I personally think that Scouting is a great organization, and not just because I learned to masturbate at summer camp. They do a great job in teaching outdoor skills and in preparing kids to be good citizens, but they fail their membership, both youths and adults, when it comes to sex. They are not alone. Schools, churches, and doctors "educate" many more kids badly about sex than do the Scouts. I feel let down by all of them.

Working with sex offenders made it very clear to me that

masturbation and fantasy are critical in the development of sexual turn-ons. I met a youth leader who admitted that he sexually molested the kids in his care. He had always masturbated to the fantasy of sex with young boys. As a sex therapist, it is also clear to me that masturbation can be a powerful treatment modality. The problem with masturbation as a therapeutic tool is in getting people to use it. I've often wished that there were a book I could recommend to help deal with that reluctance and negativity.

Personally and professionally frustrated about societal attitudes about sex and masturbation, I was also in the process of dealing with midlife transitions. It is now clear to me that all of these are related. Midlife is a natural time of change and reflection. It's certainly not the only time, but is the one with which I most clearly identify. By middle age, most men have learned about the physical, genital aspects of sexuality and are now open to the emotional, sensual aspects as well. Middle-aged women may have the emotional part down, and now want the physical part as well. Unfortunately, most of us in midlife share a strong sense of shame and guilt about sexuality in general and masturbation in particular. Masturbation thus becomes a prism through which we can examine both our sexuality and our masculinity/femininity.

I believe that the way we masturbate reflects our view of ourselves as men and women in our society. We get the job done. It is usually not a positive emotional experience. If we want to get out of our stereotyped power-and-control relationships and focus on intimacy and feelings, then we have to change our masturbatory habits. In order to understand why this is so, we have to understand the paradox of being men in a patriarchal society. Men may have the power, but we don't have the feelings. We are winners and losers, oppressors and oppressed, victors and victims, the privileged and the dispossessed. Realizing that a part is missing can be a major motivating factor in life transitions. It certainly has been for me. That's what I mean by moving "beyond friction," beyond the basic piston mechanics of masturbation to an exploration and acceptance of the associated feelings and emotions. Only after we know and accept ourselves can we be truly present in a sexual-emotional connection with another person.

So far, it might appear that women don't masturbate. Obviously they do; however, not as many do and not as often as men. While I am foursquare in favor of gender equality in masturbation, I don't believe that the issues are the same for men and women. The original concern about masturbation was in the wasting of seed and/or vital fluid, not in having an unassisted orgasm. Early church fathers probably didn't even know that women *had* orgasms, assisted or unassisted. Most believed that women had no seed to spill, and no one has ever been able to link female orgasm with fertility. For most early medical writers, vaginal secretion was not considered as vital a fluid as semen. In the context of sex for procreation only, women have had to contend with masculine negativity about birth control and especially about abortion. The masturbation proscription pales in comparison.

Having said that, I hasten to add that shame and guilt are equal opportunity negative emotions for both men and women who masturbate. Negative attitudes toward sex as pleasure apply equally to both sexes.

It is a paradox of sorts that women masturbate less frequently but discuss it more openly than men do. There are already at least three good handbooks (no pun intended) out there that encourage women to masturbate in pursuit of positive and pleasurable sexuality. I know of no such book for men.

Some feminists might argue that no man should tell them how or why to masturbate. I would not presume to do so. There are many common elements in the history of sex negativity and they apply to women as well as to men.

This book presents the material that I know to be helpful in the process of changing our attitudes toward masturbation. I've tried to tell this story using experiences of men and women who are struggling, but we need to know our collective history as well. We have to understand how psychology, sociology, anthropology, statistics, anatomy, physiology, medicine, religion, and education have viewed sex and masturbation over time. Many of us have to work an issue through cognitively and rationally before we can accept it emotionally. Only then do we consider changing our personal values. Cognitive negativity and emotional discomfort have delivered a one-two punch to sexual pleasure, especially solitary sexual pleasure. For many of us, masturbation feels good physically and bad emotionally.

In the last chapter, I will suggest a path to travel in order to get in touch with your personal sense of sexuality. I hope that you will be willing to try some alternative pathways on this journey of exploration to the Dark Continent of emotion and sensuality.

As a man, I've tried to get a hold on the relationship between man and penis. Beyond the basic qualification of masculinity, I have other credentials for commenting on man and his primary tool. I grew up in a conservative, Republican, New England family and community, a Catholic with Ivy League training in psychology, a medical degree, and biological training in psychiatry. I've been certified in both psychiatry and sex therapy, and I've probably heard all the negative sexual messages known to man. On the other hand, because of that extensive therapeutic experience, I've heard many positive messages about sexuality as well. Some people have even said good things about masturbation. As I journey through my fifties, I try to reframe my view of life based on how it really is and how I would really like it to be rather than how I was taught that it was supposed to be. Masturbation can be a vehicle for that change. I'd like to be able to carry a sign in support of the surgeon general, proclaim that "I'm Proud to Pound My Pud," and tell the middle-aged lady pollster at the door that I jerked off twice last week. I want to feel good about masculinity, midlife, masturbation, sexuality, and social roles.

It's taken several years to put these ideas down in a systematic way. For two of those years, I lived and worked in New Zealand. That accounts for the "down under" references. It also taught me that some folks have a very long way to go in coming to terms with sexuality.

I invite you to share in this journey beyond friction. In the process of change, the Republican Party, the National Rifle Association, and the Catholic Church have lost at least one member. The beat goes on.

NOTES

1. Kaye Wellings, Julia Field, Anne Johnson, et al., *Sexual Behaviour in Britain* (London: Penguin, 1994).

2. Edward Laumann, John Gagnon, Robert Michael, et al., *The Social Organization of Sexuality* (Chicago: University of Chicago Press, 1994).

3. Robin Baker, *Sperm Wars: The Science of Sex* (New York: Basic Books, 1996).

4. Edward Rowan, "Masturbation According to the Boy Scout Handbook," *Journal of Sex Education and Therapy* 15 (1989): 77–81.

Chapter One

∎

The Task

∎

M an has a very complex relationship with his penis. It provides pain and pleasure, joy and sorrow, and it often has a mind of its own. One of the first things that all of us heard about this relationship in our families, communities, schools, and churches was that man should keep his hands off his penis. The masturbation taboo is an ancient one and a critical element in how each and every one of us has developed as a sexual being. Despite—or sometimes because of—the taboo, most of us masturbated anyway. Masturbation was basic training for all the advanced work we did in sexuality. Masturbation is common ground. It is an experience we all share but one about which surprisingly (or not so surprisingly) little has been written.

Women also have a complex relationship with their genitals. This starts with "What do you call it down there?" Masturbation requires stimulation, direct or indirect, of the clitoris, but many women have never seen theirs and some don't know it exists. A general term for the female genitals is elusive: "pudenda" is pedantic, "vulva" sounds like a Swedish sedan, "vagina" is only partially anatomically correct, and "cunt" may be okay for feminists but not for male writers. The phraseology will just have to evolve as we go along.

It's hard to talk about masturbation. Almost every one of us has done it and many of us continue to do it. Almost all of us feel guilty about it. While rationally we know that it doesn't hurt us and actually feels good, we still insist that the next generation not do it. When men describe it, we use aggressive terms, but "real men" aren't supposed to do it. When we want to instill moral discipline, we renounce the pleasure in it (see chapter 6); when we want to therapeutically change behavior, we reinforce that pleasure (see chapter 11). It's a paradox. How can something that makes us feel so good make us feel so bad?

Once upon a time, early in our lives, masturbation was fun. With a young child's sense of wonder, we discovered pleasure in our bodies: sucking, defecating, and playing with our genitals. All of it felt good. Unfortunately, most of us don't remember any of it, but we've probably seen it in our own or other children. To wax scientific for a moment, the neurons in the temporal lobe of the brain where memories are stored were not myelinated yet. More simply stated, the wires weren't insulated yet, and conscious memories of pleasure were not recorded and stored by our brains. After the wiring was completed, at about age three, we did lay down memory traces. We were then made aware of other peoples' responses to our pleasures and socialized, as it were, to conform to the rules. Like puppies trained not to poop on the rug, we were trained not to play with our pricks or clits. Sometimes the same roll of newspaper was used: whack the puppy, whack the kid. Same principle.

In some primitive societies, life is simpler. It's all right for kids to play, and this includes playing with themselves. At the end of childhood, the now-pubescent male adolescent is welcomed into the world of men by enduring some ritual. He gets a totem, a new name, and permission to have sex. Female adolescents get their period and permission to be pregnant.

In industrialized societies, the rites of passage are much more complex. Adolescence has become synonymous with prolonged education and training. We mark time and delay having children until we have real jobs. Delaying procreation often means the avoidance of any form of sexual expression, including masturbation. The task is a hopeless one, given raging hormones and increased sexual tension. Unfortunately, the attitudes and behaviors instilled by the powers that be and learned at this time of life often continue beyond adolescence and haunt us throughout adulthood.

"The powers that be" are the patriarchal voices of power and control. They have religious, medical, and moral authority behind them, and they do not relinquish power easily. For example, the press recently reported that a cardinal had denounced homosexuals and said that they could not march in the St. Patrick's Day parade. But according to the New Catechism, the fornicators and masturbators must be eliminated as well. This would leave a very short parade, consisting mostly of self-propelled green baby carriages.

A few of us may challenge the sexual stereotypes earlier in life, but almost all of us revisit them at midlife. Midlife transitions are real. They are defined not so much by age as by changing events. Midlife is a time of change in family, work, and physical status. Parents are dying, children are leaving, and spouses are taking on new roles. Work status is assessed relative to early goals, and shrinking possibilities may have to be acknowledged. Physical vulnerabilities and the aging process are apparent. Midlife as a transition period may require a simple "course correction" or may reach the level of "crisis." It includes coming to terms with physical changes and reassessing vocational progress. The male and female stereotypes that men "do" and women "feel" must also be reconsidered.

Physical changes go beyond a chrome dome and a beer belly to the realization that we have passed our physical peaks. Not only will we never play third base for the Red Sox, but we have also started that long slide into old age, which may end in infirmity and senility. Similarly, we now know that we're not like to get off the production line, beyond middle management, or into a seat of wealth and power. We have to decide to hang in until retirement, chuck the whole thing and work on the great American novel, or accept ourselves as we are. For many people, whatever they have done has not been enough. It may be time for a change.

An ensuing sense of isolation may result in bonding behaviors as we find others who feel as we do, and new mentors may become important. This time it may be a guru with inner peace rather than a CEO with an ulcer. As part of the feeling revolution, we may reconsider sexual repression and sexual stereotypes and, hopefully, reexperience good feelings, including the wonders associated with childhood. This then becomes a mythic midlife journey away from friction-based sexuality and toward personal pleasure and individual control.

This is also the new male psychology, which is not to be confused with the old male-oriented psychology or the new feminist psychology. A century ago, Sigmund Freud formulated "psychodynamic" psychology. His concept of psychic causality, that we do everything for a reason, is still fundamental; however, Freud did not understand women. He based his theory of sexual normality on the appropriate resolution of the "Oedipal complex." According to this theory, boys have to stop trying to win their mothers, acknowledge the power of their fathers, and wait to find women of their own. Conversely, women had to stop trying to win their fathers and wait for men of their own. It is important to note that failure to "resolve" this conflict and to take on the exclusive role of dominant heterosexual male or passive heterosexual female was considered to be a "perversion." Freud wrote about "castration anxiety" in little boys and "penis envy" in little girls.[1] How every kid in the world became familiar with his or her anatomy and that of the opposite sex is unclear. Not every boy fears his penis will be cut off, nor does every girl wish she had one. Freud was bound up in his own society, a patriarchal Jewish family in upper-middle-class Victorian Vienna. He believed that anatomy was destiny. He never seemed to understand the difficulty of generalizing his culturally bound, male-oriented psychology to the whole human race.

It is said that Freud himself was open to new ideas and he did, in fact, change some of his theories during his lifetime. Unfortunately, they were set in concrete when he died. I once had a professor who started a lecture by intoning, "As Father Freud once said. . . ." The gospel according to Saint Sigmund is that females and perverts are inferior and both lack power and control.

"Feminine psychology" is a term coined by Karen Horney in 1967.[2] She agreed with Freud about psychic causality but disagreed vehemently with his ideas about femininity. She saw male and female principles as natural and complementary rather than oppositional and superior/inferior: Men were objective and women, subjective. Horney thought that males envied the physiological superiority of motherhood and that they feared menstruation, vaginal containment, and the inadequacy of a small penis. Men would therefore choose infantile, nonmaternal, and hysterical women in order to perpetuate their stereotypes. She believed that male objectivity may have had something to do with the ability of males to see their external genitalia while female introspection and subjectivity were related to hidden internal genitals. Despite this, it was social conditioning and not anatomy that was destiny.

Following up on this formulation of "womb envy," subsequent proponents of the new feminist psychology such as Carol Gilligan have clarified the differences between the sexes and assigned them different values. Assuming that most children in our society are raised by their mothers, then the gender identity task for most boys is to separate and for most girls, it is to attach. For boys, separation and individuation are associated with such characteristics as competition, autonomy, achievement, and attention to rules and responsibility. For girls, attachment is associated with cooperation, caring, concern, and attention to relationships. Gilligan argues that it is the latter that represents real human strength. Males have problems with intimacy and relationships, while females have problems with separation and individuation.[3] Men in midlife begin to see the importance of intimacy, relationships, and caring, while women have always known that these things were important.

If there had not been a women's movement away from the stereotypes of power and control as "normal," then there would not have been a new male psychology of non-traditional behaviors and values. There would have been no intensive study of what is now called "masculine gender-role conflict" as a result of the "male role socialization process." Both Robert Bly and Sam Keen offer us a path to midlife resolution. Their respective works, titled *Iron John* and *Fire in the Belly*, suggest a journey: First separate from tradition and stereotypes, and then live in a world of men. Here, there is initiation by a mentor and an inner journey to get back in touch with the wild man within.

Bly sees one important midlife task as the reintegration of sexuality and spirituality. The sexual instinct has traditionally been learned as troublesome and hostile to the spirit and it must be reclaimed as a valued, positive part of the self.[4] Keen similarly sees the traditional focus of sexuality as an erect penis prepared for war and work (power and control.) The penile warrior must be recaptured, pacified, and enlightened about true intimacy.[5]

Sexuality in general and masturbation in particular are metaphors for the new male psychology. We must take the mythic journey back to the time when masturbation was pleasurable and value-free, see how it became encumbered with the values of power and control, and then try to reconnect with the repressed good feelings about the male body and the male self. It may actually be true that a men's group drumming and bonding in the woods is a metaphorical circle jerk or that a hero's journey is a masturbatory fantasy. We must discover how the "evils" of masturbation are connected to the myths of power and control and how our unquestioning silence promotes these myths.

If masturbation is normal, natural, and necessary, then why do we feel so bad about it? To begin to understand this, we must first look to early learning experiences. One of these is education. Currently there are over twelve hundred published sex education curricula available in the United States. A few of them even mention masturbation. Unfortunately, most students have not been exposed to sex education or have not have been enlightened if they were. Ideally, as teenagers we should have read Dr. Eleanor Hamilton, who wrote that "the only consequence of masturbation is feeling unnecessarily guilty."[6] Sol Gordon wrote that "each person finds a level that is satisfying and gratifying and there are no ill effects."[7] Now, I didn't learn that in my school. In reality, my high school biology teacher was really excited about a quart of squash bugs and cucumber beetles and passed them around the room. She also took the human reproduction pages out of our workbooks because "the girls would be uncomfortable." Given the extent of their negative responses to the bugs, it is difficult to imagine how the girls would have responded to the subject of sex. That would have been really disgusting. Certainly, the teacher said nothing about masturbation. My Scout Handbook told me not to excite emissions but to do the manly thing and practice conservation. The priest told me that it was a mortal sin if I played with myself and to save "it" for marriage. He didn't say how many jars that might take. The home medical advisor suggested that it would lead to pimples and lack of energy. My doctor didn't offer any information and I didn't ask. I kept jerking off despite the warnings. A lot of us did. We remained silent, guilty, ashamed, ignorant, and powerless, but we kept on coming.

Others have had different experiences. Over the years, many have shared their life stories with me. Often they talk about masturbation: how they did it, what it meant, and how they felt. Like me, they marvel at the effects it had and continues to have on their lives.

Mike, a thirty-nine-year-old engineer: "One night when I was about twelve, I was lying in bed on my stomach. I don't remember what I was thinking about but I got a hard-on and started rubbing back and forth on the bed. When all that stuff came out, I was scared and thought I'd hurt myself. I didn't tell anyone. A week or so later the same thing happened. It felt pretty good but I thought that there must be something wrong. I kept doing it but I was convinced that somehow I was hurting myself. I really felt guilty and was confused because my mother washed the sheets and must have seen the stains but she never said a word. I almost wanted her to say something so I could confess and she could reassure me. I still feel guilty about it."

Alan, a forty-five-year-old lawyer: "We were at Scout Camp and one of the older kids said that he wanted to show us something. He was pumping his hand up and down his cock. He called it jerking off. "What's all that wet stuff?" I asked after a while. "Try it and see," he suggested. I did but it didn't work. He said that it would help the cock grow and he had a really big one so I kept trying. Finally it came. It was really neat and I kept doing it. He was wrong though; I'm forty-five, and I still haven't made it grow as big as his. I still wish I had a bigger cock."

Sandra, a thirty-four-year-old artist: "It was a wonderfully liberating experience to attend a workshop for 'preorgasmic women.' We undressed and looked at our bodies and got comfortable in touching ourselves. We learned the most effective ways to arouse pleasurable feelings and experimented with hands and vibrators. That first orgasm was absolutely thrilling. My partner was reluctant to do what I showed him and I think he was put off by the idea that I could have fun without him."

Tom, a forty-two-year-old policeman: "I sat up front in the third grade and the teacher's desk was on a raised platform. I looked right at her legs and she wore stockings and heels. I thought about her all the time. I'm not sure if there's a connection but today I like to imagine myself in nylons and heels, not fishnets, but smooth and silky pantyhose with black pumps. Just thinking about it gets me aroused. When I put them on at home, I get a hard-on and I like to rub myself through the pantyhose. It's better than sex with my wife."

Ursula, a seventy-seven-year-old retired teacher: "It was very strange for me growing up. My mother would put mittens on my hands when I went to bed and insist that they stay outside the covers. I knew I was not supposed to touch myself but I didn't understand why. She slapped my face when my period started and never said that it was supposed to be for good luck. She never said much beyond how to keep from staining my clothes. It was years before I understood that touching myself and bleeding were not connected. I never thought that sex was pleasurable. It was a job that had to be done."

Ron, a forty-six-year-old state prison inmate: "For years I drew pictures of a little girl with a hairless pussy and just nipple buds. Then I'd jerk off. I've had sex with girls like that and that's why I'm here. The counselor tells me to think about grown-up women, but I still have to have that picture in mind every time I get off."

Beth, a thirty-one-year-old graduate student: "When I was little, my mother's boyfriend used to sit me on his lap and put his hand in my panties. He would rub me and say he was helping me feel good. It didn't, but I was afraid to tell him to stop. Any kind of sexual touching is still really hard for me."

Alex, a forty-year-old carpenter: "As a boy, I shared a room with my older sister. I liked to watch her dress and undress and eventually masturbated under the covers while I watched. One day she caught me and wanted to see what I was doing. It was an incredible turn-on for both of us, so we watched each other for a couple of years until she went away to school. Watching my wife dress and undress is still my favorite turn-on."

Ted, a thirty-six-year-old pilot: "One day I was in the garage jerking off and wondered what it would be like to be penetrated. I stuck a basketball needle into the hole in my dick. I pushed the pump handle, and the cold, stabbing feeling really scared me. The penetration itself was really exciting. I never pushed cold air in again, but I've been inserting larger and larger things into my ass and dick. The sensation is wonderful."

Irv, a forty-year-old teacher: "I really like doing myself. It can take hours. I go very slowly and use massage oil, which I rub all over my cock. I like to tease myself right up to the edge and then stop. After several of those, I have a powerful come that makes me want to yell, it feels so good. Nobody can make love to me the way I can."

Owen, a forty-four-year-old insurance salesman: "I never touched myself as a kid because I knew it was a sin. I saved myself for marriage. My wife was a virgin, too. Sex was never any fun so we stopped after the boys were born. We're very busy with church and don't miss it."

Nick, a thirty-year-old computer technician: "We try to be very open with our six-year-old daughter and to answer her questions about sex. We've told her that it is perfectly normal to touch herself and to masturbate. Last night she started doing it at the dinner table. I didn't know what to do but I said, 'That's for private places,' and that was all there was to it. Was that the right thing to do?"

Ray, a sixty-eight-year-old retired physician: "My wife had cancer surgery and she just isn't interested in sex anymore. I have to take care of myself. We've never talked about it , but she probably knows. As long as I don't bother her, it seems OK. I wish it could be different."

Uri, a forty-seven-year-old social worker: "I really like oral sex, but I don't have a partner. I do have a Labrador Retriever with a huge tongue. I smear butter on my cock and I've taught her to lick it off. What a feeling. Sometimes I worry that she'll nuzzle my crotch in public, but I think it's the butter she goes for."

Lee, a twenty-five-year-old secretary: "I first discovered the pleasure of masturbation in the bathtub. I had this hand-held shower gizmo and when I first sprayed my clit, it was like, wow! A good come is a great way to relax and I can take care of myself after a really tough day at work."

Edgar, a thirty-three-year-old cab driver: "The guys in school were talking about beating off. I went home and beat my prick against my leg until it hurt. What's the big deal? Next day I saw my friend with a funny, guilty look on his face. He said he just beat off. I told him I did too but it just hurt. He must have thought I was pretty stupid because he had to show me what to do."

Sam, a fifty-four-year-old writer: "I would lock the bathroom door and sit on the toilet. Then I'd write her name in hair oil on my prick and beat off. She was the prettiest girl in school but I was too shy to ask her out and she was the wrong religion anyway. Those fantasies were as close as I ever got to her. Funny, my ex-wife and the last woman I dated looked a lot like her."

These vignettes may or may not be problems. They are experiences with masturbation, each of which has had a profound effect on at least one person's intimacy and sexuality. I do know that none of these is unique. Later we will revisit some of these people and meet others as we explore where the focus on friction has led us and where we aspire to go in the future.

NOTES

1. See Charles Brenner, *An Elementary Textbook of Psychoanalysis* (Garden City: Doubleday, 1955), chap. 5.

2. Karen Horney, *Feminine Psychology* (New York: W. W. Norton, 1967).

3. Carol Gilligan, *In a Different Voice* (Cambridge: Harvard University Press, 1982).

4. Robert Bly, *Iron John* (Reading, Mass.: Addison-Wesley, 1990).

5. Sam Keen, *Fire in the Belly* (New York: Bantam, 1991).

6. Eleanor Hamilton, *Sex with Love* (Boston: Beacon Press, 1978).

7. Sol Gordon, *The Teenage Survival Book* (New York: Times Books, 1988).

Chapter Two

Laying the Foundation

I n order for us to understand the evolution of our sexuality, we need to make three basic assumptions about the
human condition. The first is that sexual arousal and orgasm feel good. While we have no objective proof of this
pleasure, we see the smiles, we hear the moans, we're told
that it feels good, and we have our own personal experiences. There is a great deal of subjective evidence to render
the assumption of pleasure valid. There is no body of evidence to suggest that arousal and orgasm feel bad or that
they are generally reported to be painful, uncomfortable, or
without sensation at all, although individual exceptions do
exist.

The second assumption is that the good feelings that
result from sexual arousal logically reinforce whatever
behavior produced that pleasure. Such "positive reinforcement" is a basic tenet of behavioral psychology. Unlike the
"negative reinforcement" of touching a hot stove, the positive experiences are repeated. "If it feels good, do it" then
becomes the motto of the young child who operates on the
"pleasure principle." As children, we discover the pleasure

of sexual feelings long before we learn that the biological function of these feelings is to prepare for reproduction of the species. Even if we have a talk about the "birds and bees," we probably don't associate that story with the sexual feelings we experience. What does pollinating a flower have to do with touching a penis or some other pleasurable place that we have discovered? The more primitive emotional experience of pleasure certainly precedes the intellectual understanding of the true purpose of sexuality. We all know that it is still difficult to move beyond our emotional responses to be logical and objective about a powerful experience.

The third assumption is more complex. If sex feels good and if good feelings reinforce associated behaviors, then why not just do it? Elementary sociology teaches us that as people banded together in societies in order to diversify labor, a structure emerged and rules evolved. Individual pleasure was no longer primarily important. A hierarchy of authority developed. Societal organization was preferable to the breakdown and chaos assumed to be inherent in the individual pursuit of pleasure. Individual pleasure and power were harnessed in the service of the greater good. A corollary of this is that one of the first freedoms to be repressed in an authoritarian state is sexual freedom.

One of the first rules promulgated in any society is the one regulating sexual expression. While the purpose of sex may be the continuation of the species, there are some potential sex partners who are off-limits for social and/or political reasons. One example of this is the prohibition of sex between family or clan members, so that the women remained valuable virgins for marriage in order to receive a dowry or form alliances with other clans. We know that this "incest taboo" may have some biological as well as political advantages; however, the ancients were not up to speed on genetic linkages. Other examples are rules or conventions against sex and other relationships with lower castes or social classes. Children must be taught the rules of the group: forego personal pleasure for the greater good of the society and be selective in the object and/or method of sexual expression. Thus the basic ambivalence is created: Sex is good but it can be bad.

Authority, be it religious or secular, cannot always be present in order to point out every bad act or violation of the societal code. It can put forth the idea that what is bad—a legal or moral error—should produce a sense of guilt. Socialization requires that such violations of the rules produce guilt in the absence of a policeman at the elbow and the finding of guilt in a court of law. One must internalize the rule that bad behaviors will be punished and self-impose guilt over infractions. Guilt's partner is shame. When the real self deviates from the idealized self in adhering to the norms of society, these discrepancies produce shame. You know what you should have done. In the United States, the roadside signs say, "$100 fine for littering." In Australia and New Zealand they say, "Do the right thing, don't litter." The former is guilt and the latter, shame. Guilt and shame, then, become the mental police at one's elbow who enforce the rules. Feeling wrong and not measuring up can be more powerful enforcers than a couple of guys who threaten to break your kneecaps if you break society's rules.

In addition to forbidding pleasure in the pursuit of discipline, rule-making authority may also try to control the sexual mission of males. Sperm has the power to make babies and it ought to be saved for the proper female receptacles. The female receptacles aren't supposed to interfere with the procreative power of the sperm. Harnessing the power of procreation harnesses the power of sexuality. We will return to this idea later, but it is clearly an additional motivation for control of both sexes.

In summary then, sexual arousal is pleasurable and it can lead to the even more pleasurable sensation of orgasm. However, internalized societal rules place limits on the expression of that pleasure, and they create shame and guilt when the rules are broken. Sex feels physically good but it feels emotionally bad.

Attitudes about masturbation have come to symbolize the societal prohibition of sexuality. If pleasure can be experienced alone, then denial and control of that pleasure become models for the authoritarian imposition of self-discipline in the pursuit of larger societal goals. Contrary to our self-centered frame of reference, Western ideas about sexuality in general and masturbation in particular do not represent a universal norm. Not only are there cross-cultural differences in attitudes about masturbation and variations within our own culture, but there has been an evolution within this culture as well. Generally speaking, the prohibition was first couched in religious terms, then in "scientific" medical terms, and then in moralistic terms. Unfortunately for us, all of these continue to exist to some degree today, and individuals still report sin, sickness, and shame as results of their solitary pleasure.

Most of our early masturbatory experiences had multiple meanings. There was intuitive pleasure and sensuality. There was a feeling of power and self-control. There was a message of guilt and shame. As young children, we first masturbated for pure pleasure and later to control sexual tension, once we figured out what it was and how to relieve it. We usually discovered the pleasure ourselves (88 percent of men and 82 percent of women in one recent survey[1]) but sometimes, someone else told us about it or showed us how to do it. Adults, however enlightened, gave us the message that it was wrong. Even if parents thought it was natural, what would the teacher say if a kid did it for show and tell? If there were no spoken words about sin, sickness, or shame, then it was obvious by the body language that the behavior was unacceptable. Consider the shocked look, the disappointed shrug, the bitten lip, the pained expression, or the mantle of failure as a good mother. It was a rare parent indeed who indicated verbally and demonstrated nonverbally that masturbation was truly normal and natural.

As adolescents, we learned that the behavior that felt good also had competitive value. Many men will remember the circle jerk. For the uninitiated, this consists of a group of adolescent males in roughly circular formation, jerking off together. Circle jerks and pissing contests were not for pleasure, but to identify a winner who was the fastest, who could shoot the farthest, the most frequently, or with the most accuracy. Pissing contests were for distance or duration and rarely for artistic endeavor. Writing your name in the snow was simply proof that you were the winner. Circle jerks were one of the earliest forms of male bonding. Just us guys being male and playing with our tools. We thought that the best guy got off first; after all, it was pursuit of the orgasm that was the goal. Those who excelled in long distance and accuracy were the more athletically inclined; those guys also wanted to hit home runs and score touchdowns. Older kids also demonstrated techniques to uninitiated younger ones. The circle jerk where everyone did the guy on the right (except for the southpaws) was unusual. It just seemed like, well, homosexuality. That didn't fit with the power image. Pleasure and sensuality were not the goals. This was a contest, not a love-in. The tools were not connected to feelings.

Martha Cornog recently reported on group masturbation in girls.[2] This occurs less frequently than for boys, happens in pairs rather than larger groups, and the games are more likely to be "playing doctor" or "playing house" than to be contests. She also notes a growing number of adult "solo sex clubs" or "jerk-off (JO) clubs" over the last twenty years. Most advertise in gay or lesbian publications. JO clubs for males have rules that forbid penetration and emphasize safe sex. Female clubs may allow more extensive sexual contact. Coed Jack-and-Jill-Off clubs exist, but are rare as the adult groups mimic exclusionary adolescent peer groups.

Adolescent male masturbation is orgasm-oriented: The thinking is concrete, the objective is to "get off." The logical extension of this goal-oriented thinking to partner sex is to focus on bringing the partner to orgasm. The goal is in the act of coming, not in the process of getting there. Total focus on orgasm takes away any sense of mutuality in the encounter and many partners feel manipulated, objectified, and controlled by the process.

Power and contests notwithstanding, the societal message to testosterone-driven adolescent males is one of control. Abstinence-based sex education tells them to control sexuality, control pleasure, and save it for marriage. Maybe a few guys listen. Paradoxically, they are constantly bombarded by the media message that "sex sells" and any thirty random seconds of MTV drive that sexual message home. Peers support the "stud" image of competitive high school sexual activity. Nothing is said in support of universal masturbation for birth control and disease prevention. Which message is the most powerful?

Adolescent girls have raging hormones, too. "Control pleasure" is the message to them as well. This is supported by the negative peer image of sexually active high school girls. The paradoxical message for them is to dress provocatively but remain virginal (technically, at least). Teenage pregnancy is shameful. Nothing is said about birth control, disease prevention, or experiencing orgasm. Girls thinking about emotional relationships are not focused on "doing it" the way that boys are.

At some point in life, for some men, change occurs and pleasure replaces competition. The tool becomes connected to feelings. They get beyond friction. They should become our mentors. For other men, the end of sex as power is the end of sex at all. "It isn't important." "I gave it up." "Old men don't do it anyway." Rationalizations, perhaps; but these messages clearly signal the end of a phase and the inability to conceptualize sex as pleasure. How do sensual men get to be sensual? How do they evolve from physical to spiritual, from getting laid to making love, from sex to sensuality?

For most, I believe, this is a result of the realization of their own vulnerability and mortality. They stop and smell the roses (or coffee if flowers are too effete.) A friend once suggested that teenage girls realize their vulnerability when they have a pelvic exam, spread-eagle in the stirrups and exposed to the world. If all teenage males were required to have a prostate exam, to bend over the table, rest on their elbows, and have a finger stuck up their butt, then they would feel vulnerable and powerless, too. I think that there's more to it than that. The family jewels have always hung out there, vulnerable and unprotected, and that doesn't make men feel any more sensual. They just buy an aluminum jock. The annual prostate exam after age forty tells us that we are vulnerable to cancer and death. An aluminum jock won't help. The same is true of major surgery and heart attacks. It is only then, after confrontation with our own mortality, that we stop to consider the pleasures of the moment. Maybe we won't get to the goal and we should pay more attention to the journey. We need to stop and listen to some of the old guys. They have been telling us for years that after age or physical illness have taken away the erection and/or the orgasm, the goal is not as important. There is pleasure in the relationship, in closeness, and in whole-body sensation. We haven't been listening to them or even observing that our female partners have been more tuned in to sensuality that we have.

Adult males need to revisit the origins of their guilt and

shame and then to restructure their values and perceptions of themselves. If the idealized self could enjoy pleasure and sensuality, there would be no discrepancy for the experience of pleasure and there would be no shame. If one could leave self-control behind with the other authoritarian power images, one could then cease being overwhelmed by the power of sexuality. It should follow that one might stop repressing it, start enjoying it for its own sake, and stop feeling guilty about it.

Women may come to this time of change from a different perspective. Many are searching for an orgasm. They may have fulfilled their job as receptacles but it didn't feel good. As one said, "I wasn't sexually active; I just lie there." They now realize that they have missed something and discover that masturbation may be the route to success.

Shame-free, guilt-free masturbation can be part of positive sexuality and sensuality. The sensual experience includes feelings of arousal and excitement as well as permission for lingering pleasure. When our masturbation is no longer goal-oriented, then we generally drop aggressive terms and start using feeling terms for it. We must also be open to a different consideration; not a codified "Thou shalt not," but a situational standard. Situational ethics simply state that the right thing to do depends on the circumstances at the time the decision is made. The classic example has always been that it is proper to lie when the Gestapo ask if you are hiding Jews in your attic. In this situation, it is ethical to lie. A contemporary example could be that masturbation is preferable to unprotected sexual activity in the age of AIDS. Imagine the ad campaign and the bumper sticker: "Masturbate—it could save your life." In this situation, it is ethical to masturbate.

There is no standard or absolute value for masturbation; it depends on the situation that we are in. Masturbation, intrinsically, is a value-free act.

With all their sexual energy directed to procreation, the ancient fathers apparently did not see, and perhaps did not care, that women were anything other the receptacles for ejaculate. Female orgasm was unnecessary for pregnancy, and the male-focused ancient fathers may never even have realized that women could be orgasmic. Their own orgasms were strictly functional and not supposed to be pleasurable anyway. The ancient mothers, as a group, were not educated enough to write learned books in order to share their experiences. They apparently kept their pleasure to themselves or talked only to other women at the cooking fire or at the well. If the ancient fathers knew, they either refused to acknowledge that women could have pleasure without them or they didn't want to encourage the practice by writing about it. Modern day opponents of sex education still think that way and argue that information implies permission rather than serving as a basis for informed decision making. Whatever the thinking, historically there has not been the preoccupation with female masturbation as there has been with male activity. There is a common threat however, the prohibition of freedom of choice in pleasure versus procreation.

Sexual freedom may be viewed as a threat to the existing social order. Some worry that it is associated with the breakdown of hierarchy and authority and a descent into anarchy and chaos. Anarchy and chaos are not seen as a celebration of choice, positive change, independent thinking, individual rights, or personal freedom, but rather as a loss of control by those holding power. This view cannot conceptualize "anarchy" as mediated by the Golden Rule where individuals "do the right thing" to each other so it can be done unto them in the same way. The only sexual choices are those approved by the hierarchy. Control of masturbation and pregnancy becomes the focus of authoritarian control of sexual freedom. Independent orgasm and independent thought are both threats to that authority.

If ignorance is bliss, and if silence promotes ignorance, then there is little wonder that those in authority do not want to talk about sexual freedom. In their view, we should stay dumb and happy.

NOTES

1. Harold Leitenberg, Mark Detzer, and Debra Srebnick, "Gender Differences in Masturbation and the Relation of Masturbatory Experience in Preadolescence and/or Early Adolescence to Sexual Behavior and Sexual Adjustment in Young Adulthood," *Archives of Sexual Behavior* 22 (1993): 87–98.

2. Martha Cornog, "The Circle Game: Social Masturbation for Young and Old(er)," paper presented at the Midwest Chapter of the Society for the Scientific Study of Sexuality, Madison, Wis., 1999. Her *Big Book on Masturbation* will be published by Down There Press in winter 2000.

Chapter Three

—■—

Thoughts, Words, and Deeds

—■—

Before we go any further, we must be sure that we are all talking about the same thing—masturbation. The word is derived from the Latin *manu struprare* meaning "to defile by hand" or *masturbari* meaning "to defile oneself." The word apparently evolved as "manustrupate" to "mastuprate" to "masturbate" by the nineteenth century. There are many other words and phrases out there. Over the years, we collected terms in college classes. These students were generally middle-class and white. Friends and neighbors in New Zealand generously contributed the Anglo-Kiwi perspective. The masculine terms include: jack off, jerk off, toss off, beat the meat, choke the chicken, beat the baron, hand slag, hand job, play with yourself, wank the willy, pound the pud, cuff the dummy, whack the weenie, flog the log, slam the ham, pump it 'til it pukes, shake hands with the unemployed, strum the string, play pocket pool, hood the bishop, spank the monkey, slake the bacon, whizz the jizz, date Rosy Palm and her five little sisters, whip the wire, yank the crank, unclog the pipes, and burp the worm. This is not poetry in motion but rather a violent-sounding activity, in various combinations and permutations, done to the bald-headed hermit, bushwhacker, cock, dick, din-galing, dink, dipstick, dong, dork, eel, gun, ham, hog, hot dog, lingam, log, love muscle, love pistol, meat, member, middle leg, pecker, pee-pee, peter, phallus, pig, pole, pork sword, prick, private, pud, putz, rod, rocket, root, salami, schlong, schmuck, schwanz, short arm, snake, stalk, thing, thruster, tool, trouser trout, tube steak, violator, wand, wanger, wazoo, weapon, weenie, wee-wee, whammer, willy, worm, or penis. The aggressive, power- and control-oriented phrases are not coincidental.

In contrast with this, some men and/or their partners have pet names for the penis. Little Tom, Dick, or Harry—or whatever the owner's name is—is common. Winston tastes good, Houdini disappears, or Lazarus rises. The little brain rules. Affection seems to preclude aggression here.

The religious and early medical literature was, and still is, laden with moral condemnation with reference to the Sin of Onan, secret vice, solitary sin, pollution, venery, self-abuse, and murder in the night. "Playing with yourself" implies social and emotional immaturity. Autoeroticism, although a bit clinical, is a more neutral term. Only recently have we begun to see more positive terms such as getting off alone, ménage à moi, solitary pleasure, celebrate the self, self-gratification, solo sex, sex for one, self-loving, self-pleasing rituals, monosexualism, and auto-authentication.

When women masturbate, they don't assault their organs in the way that men do. Their methods are different, and the differences go beyond the obvious anatomical ones. While some women may use a masculine term such as "jacking off"—or the analogous "jilling off" or "flicking the clit"—for want of better words, they are much more likely to avoid the assaultive terms completely and to simply say that they play with themselves, finger, get off, masturbate, or self-pleasure. Other terms like playing with the little man in the boat, riding the curl, caressing the kitty, polishing the pearl, petting the pussy, parting the petals, tickling the fancy, and many references to Southern comfort are equally nonviolent.

Stimulation of the penis or clitoris leads to a sexual response. This appears to be straightforward. The level of sexual excitement rises until it reaches a threshold where the orgasm/ejaculation is triggered. But reality is always more complex than it appears.

One way to frame these phenomena is in terms of the "Sexual Response Cycle." First proposed by sex researchers William Masters and Virginia Johnson in 1966 as stages of Excitement and Orgasm,[1] it was modified by Helen Singer Kaplan in 1979 to add Desire preceding the Excitement and Orgasm stages.[2] Basically, the model applies to both sexes.

FIGURE 3.1: SEXUAL RESPONSE CYCLE

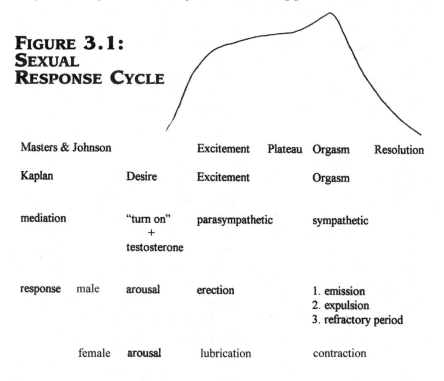

		Excitement	Plateau	Orgasm	Resolution
Masters & Johnson		Excitement	Plateau	Orgasm	Resolution
Kaplan	Desire	Excitement		Orgasm	
mediation	"turn on" + testosterone	parasympathetic		sympathetic	
response male	arousal	erection		1. emission 2. expulsion 3. refractory period	
female	arousal	lubrication		contraction	

Desire, or early arousal, has the psychological components of experience and expectation and hormonal components as well. Testosterone level is correlated with the degree of arousal in both men and women. It is unclear if this is cause-and-effect; a feedback loop in which excitement increases testosterone, which increases excitement, which increases testosterone, and so forth; or a situation in which the level of both is mediated by some as yet unknown third factor. This phase is one of being mentally "turned on" in preparation for and in anticipation of the "hard-wired" and "hydraulic" events to follow.

Excitement is that phase of response mediated by the parasympathetic nervous system. The phase events are female vaginal lubrication or "sweating" and male erection. Erection results from a complex balance of constriction and expansion. The spongelike *corpus cavernosa* fill with blood; the mechanism is *not* a simple clamping off of outflow with pooling behind the dam, however, as the blood continues to circulate. Masters and Johnson originally spoke of a "plateau phase" of excitement, suggesting that erection is a steady state prior to the next phase of orgasm. Erections, in fact, "ebb and flow" with excitement, but there is generally a buildup toward the threshold of orgasm.

The principal part of orgasm is the sympathetically mediated spasm of the pelvic musculature, primarily the pubococcygeal muscles. The 0.8 second interval is the same for men and women; however, there are differences. For men, the orgasm has two components, the first a spasm of the seminal vesicles, a signal known as "ejaculatory inevitability," and the second, the muscle spasm which forces out the ejaculate. This is usually followed by detumescence (loss of erection) and a period of time known as the "refractory period" wherein it is impossible to reinitiate the cycle of erection and ejaculation. There is tremendous individual variation in this and one major determining factor is age. Adolescents may be ready to repeat in minutes while elderly men may have to wait for days. For women, there is no refractory period, and they are therefore capable of multiple orgasms. Preliminary data suggest that prepubertal males may also have a high frequency of multiorgasmic response, but the mechanism is unknown. Women are more likely to sense orgasm as a whole-body experience than are men. Orgasm is an emotional experience as well as a physical one and, as such, it is also mediated by the limbic system of the brain, hence the claim that the brain is the primary sex organ.

The cycle is the same, regardless of what drives it. There is no internal differentiation between masturbation and sexual intercourse. Using the cycle as a model, one can better understand the problems that may occur in sexual response. The effects of drugs on testosterone levels and on parasympathetic and sympathetic centers are clearer, as are the roles of fear and anxiety. Most studies of drug effects have used male subjects; however, a growing literature suggests that women have similar adverse reactions to many medications.

The central nervous system is hierarchical and represents increasing evolutionary sophistication. The most primitive, so-called vegetative level is controlled or mediated by the parasympathetic nervous system. The next level, the "fight-or-flight" part, is mediated by the sympathetic nervous system. The highest part, the brain or cerebrum, mediates emotion via the limbic system, and cognition and thinking via the cortex. Events at one level can be overriden by events at a higher level. Parasympathetic relaxation is overriden by sympathetic fear or cerebral anxiety. Ancient man had to feel secure in his cave in order to relax, digest his food, copulate with his mate, draw on the walls, or play with his tools. If a saber-toothed tiger looked in at the cave entrance, then man was afraid and had to be prepared to run or to defend himself. This was not a time to relax and play. If he only thought that he heard a tiger or just worried that there might be tigers in the neighborhood, that anxiety would trigger the same fight-or-flight response as would a real tiger, and it would be impossible for man to relax. The system has not changed. Fear and anxiety still override relaxation in both sexes.

Conversely, cognition or emotion can trigger a response at a lower level. A parasympathetic erection can be triggered reflexively by touching the genitals, or it can be triggered by the brain. The brain signals for lubrication or erection as part of the dream stage of sleep every ninety minutes and it also does so in response to thoughts and perceptions that it labels as arousing, even in small children who don't know they are "aroused." Intense sympathetic response can even trigger pubococcygeal muscle spasm without direct stimulation. The emotional experience of orgasm can then start the whole cycle over again.

Desire, excitement, and orgasm are not steady states and may also appear sequentially, simultaneously, or not at all. These complex interactions therefore make our definition of masturbation a little more difficult. The only common denominator is self-induction.

The most basic masculine techniques are "hands on." For a man, the hand holds the penis firmly or loosely and moves up and down the penile shaft. Most of us started that way. Eighty-two percent of Shere Hite's seven thousand male respondents used the "hand job."[3] A more recent survey in *Celebrate the Self* showed this group to be about evenly divided between "pullers," who stimulate on the upstroke, and "pounders," who emphasize the downstroke.[4] The grip may vary, as "pumpers" tend to encircle the shaft with the hand, while "pullers" may reach over the glans as if gripping a doorknob.

While a dry technique works well and lends itself to

spontaneity, many men prefer to lubricate. There is less potential trauma (swelling and friction from too much rubbing), more similarity to the sensation of containment, and heightened sensitivity. The latter is especially true if one is stimulating the glans or head of the penis. Such stimulation may actually be too sensitive or even painful for some men, especially those who have not been circumcised. Lubrication lends itself to techniques such as single-direction stroking and kneading the scrotum, and, most importantly, to gentleness and a focus on sensation.

Choosing lubricants is a science of its own. Elemental lubricants include water and spit. These are easily available and nonstaining. Soap in the water adds to the sensation, but soap in the eyes and soap in the urethra sting similarly. Water-soluble gels and aloe are popular. Baby powder works. Petroleum-based lubricants produce heightened sensation but don't wash out well and also break down condoms. Vegetable oils such as safflower seem ideal because they do not stain. Some men add a few drops of a "warming oil" such as cloves or wintergreen to the mix for heightened sensation. Avoid vapo-rub. Experienced explorers of kitchen cabinets have probably tried olive oil, shortening, mayonnaise, butter, margarine, and Italian dressing with variable results. (The garlic in the latter should at least keep the vampires out of your pants.)

The medicine cabinet crowd has tried petroleum jelly and hair creams. The garage set has probably experimented with various oils, preferring the lighter grades—except, perhaps, 10-W-40 in Alaska. Massage "oils" that are glycerin based may feel too slick and may wear away too quickly. Safflower oil with scent can add a particular atmosphere and flight of imagination to the masturbatory experience. Consider the thoughts that might accompany musk, sandalwood, lemon grass, or vanilla.

Perhaps because of ambivalence about touching, some

men have developed a technique of masturbation where they slap the penis back and forth between the hands with variable degrees of force. A variation on this theme is to bounce the penis on one hand. While the hand may not actually encircle the penis, the intent is obvious.

There are also a number of frankly "hands-off" techniques. Most were probably discovered serendipitously, some in the process of working out, consciously or unconsciously, an alternative to "don't touch yourself down there." The penis may be rubbed with fur or fabric for those who like a "soft" touch, or with condoms or other rubber goods for "hard" stimulation. One of these textures might be considered a "fetish" if the particular material had special meaning or association and had to be used in order for arousal to occur. Vibrators may be held against the penis for steady stimulation of variable intensity. The penis may be rubbed against the sheets or blankets while one is lying face-down on the bed. This was the second most common technique in the Hite survey as 15 percent of her male survey respondents masturbated in this way. (The remaining 3 percent were other than pounders, pumpers, pullers, and rubbers.)[5] While the origin of rubbing against the bed is probably a simple simulation of intercourse, the use of other objects including animals and people to rub against may rise to the level of a fetish and have a particular psychological meaning.

Hite surveyed female masturbators, too. Seventy-three percent stimulated the clitoral/vulvar area with a hand (some with a vibrator) while lying on their backs. Gentle, constant motion was used to identify the exact spot most sensitive to stimulation, then rapid agitation produced orgasm. The most common lubricant was vaginal secretion. Legs apart or together seemed to be a personal preference. The second most frequent technique (5.5 percent) was the same stimulation pattern while lying on the stomach. Other methods were pressing and thrusting the clitoral/vulvar area against a soft object (4 percent), pressing the thighs together rhythmically (3 percent), water massage (2 percent), and vaginal entry (1.5 percent). Eleven percent used more than one technique.[6]

Water massage of the clitoris by showerheads, bathtub faucets, and jacuzzi jets can trigger an orgasm, although the latter two require more bodily contortion for proper exposure. Achieving a proper balance of temperature and pressure produces the best results.

Vibrators are most commonly used externally on the clitoris, which may be protected by a hand or padding if direct stimulation is too intense. Good vibrators provide focused stimulation, are always ready, last for hours, and don't roll over and start snoring before they finish the job. Many women acknowledge them as their most reliable source of sexual stimulation. Models include "personal massagers" that fit in the hand; the very popular "wand" vibrators that have a long shaft with a tennis-ball-shaped head on the end; "coil operated" vibrators that look like little handheld mixers with a variety of attachments; double-headed models; and lipstick- or penis-shaped, cylindrical, battery-powered vibrators. Battery-operated models may provide insufficient stimulation to many women, especially as they get older.

A dildo is a penis-shaped object that can be inserted in the vagina. Dildos should be washable, unbreakable, and lubricated, and have no sharp edges. Many rubber penis-look-alikes are commercially available, but a variety of fruits, vegetables, candles, and battery-operated vibrators serve as well. Although zucchini and banana seeds are an unlikely source of impregnation, covering dildos with a lubricated condom helps with protection from infection as well as lubrication. Dildos are often used externally to stimulate the clitoris. When used internally, they may be pumped in and out, but they more commonly produce a sense of vaginal filling while fingers massage the clitoris to orgasm. For women with an identified Gräfenberg or "G" spot (an area of heightened sensitivity on the anterior vaginal wall), fingers or dildos can be used to stimulate that as well. A "butt plug" may be added to intensify the feeling of fullness.

Women have a built-in source of lubrication when aroused. When working up to that point or when using toys, women often use water-based lubricants; however, because of potential internal irritation, they tend not to try the panoply of lubricants with which men experiment.

For women, not touching the genitals is as likely to be a positive, integrated, whole-body experience as it is to represent a negative, "hands-off" attitude. Squeezing the thighs together, a rhythmic tightening and loosening of the anal sphincter, and stimulating a particularly sensitive area associated with erotic feelings such as a nipple, navel, or armpit would be examples of this. Some women report the ability to achieve orgasm by fantasy alone—"think off" rather than "jerk off." This seems to be rare in men (four respondents out of five thousand in Kinsey's survey, or 0.08 percent), but the potential is there.

One memorable scene in an otherwise forgettable old pornographic movie called *Sodom and Gomorrah* is that of a man sitting in a tree and sucking his own penis. (Many of us have had that fantasy.) Alfred Kinsey reported that only .25 percent of men can actually "self-fellate."[7] Many more have tried but discovered that they lacked the flexibility, and wished that the penis were about a foot longer. Countless back strains have undoubtedly been due to attempted contortions to achieve the tongue-penis connection.

Some of the intrepid male explorers of the kitchen cabinets have gone beyond lubricants to find bowls of things with which to simulate intercourse. Cup-o-Noodles apparently enjoys some popularity in Japan, while Jell-O and mashed bananas satisfy more down-home tastes. A wide range of fruits is also available, from the simple cored apple to the whole melon family. This grocery scenario is not as exhausting as it seems if one considers that pelvic thrusting into a bowl of noodles can be done on hands and knees and well as on fingers and toes. This is not football practice or basic training. For a more expensive simulation, consider the love doll, the varieties of which range from broad-based dolls with human-size vaginas, which the Japanese call "Dutch wives," to inflatable models with multiple willing orifices.[8]

Basic masturbatory techniques may be enhanced by observation. Watching oneself get off in front of a mirror is the simplest form of this. Some may extend this to masturbation in public places such as parked cars and parks, where there is added excitement in the potential of discovery. This is not to be confused with exhibitionism, where the goal is to get a response from the viewer. This masturbator does not really want to be seen as the exhibitionist does; the thrill is in the *possibility* of being seen.

Unfortunately, men have discovered many frankly dangerous ways to enhance masturbatory sensation. These include the use of various machines, the insertion of things into the penis and rectum, and asphyxiation. Some experts do not believe that these topics should be discussed in public for fear that the curious will experiment and be hurt. In reality, the vast majority of men discover autoerotic techniques on their own and they need to be warned that some of them may be dangerous. Thus, this discussion. I know of no literature about women and masturbation machines other than vibrators and electric toothbrushes, unless one also considers horses and bicycle seats. I suspect that this is less a result of masculine mechanical aptitude (read "concrete thinking") than of active feminine imagination—and no need for devices. Mechanical masturbators are available in some sex shops and by mail. They deliver a steady up-and-down motion, sometimes with an inflatable sleeve, but many consumers find them unsatisfactory and expensive. There are also many vacuum pumps, available by prescription, which may help the impotent to achieve erections. We are not talking about these devices.

The medical literature contains many reports of penile injuries caused by masturbation with a vacuum cleaner, on the theory that if a little suction feels good, a lot of suction must feel better. Most of these injuries were caused by contact with fan blades, but some penile trauma can be caused by the metal hose connection as well. While theoretically, there is less danger if a toilet paper or paper towel tube is placed on the end of the hose, this form of stimulation is definitely not recommended. It is also difficult to explain to emergency-room personnel: "I was getting out of the shower to answer the phone, tripped, and fell onto the vacuum cleaner." Right.

The surgical literature tells us that a number of items have been inserted into the urethral opening (the hole in the penile *glans*). Some are amazingly large as the list includes bulbs, ball bearings, batteries, crayons, pens, pencils, candles, matches, plastic spoon handles, spaghetti (cooked and uncooked), hair pins, steel pins, clothesline, glass rods, and wires of various size and length. The obvious problem occurs when the items break and/or don't pull out and have to be surgically removed from the urethra or bladder. There is potential for laceration, perforation, infection, and complications of the surgery. The gentle use of sterilized rods and catheters may avoid these dangers but it is preferable not to insert anything into the penis.

Other penile injuries prevent the outflow of blood and include laceration or strangulation by string, rubber bands, or tight cock rings (used to prolong erections), and injuries from insertion into bottles (broken glass) and knot holes (splinters). Cock rings that are clamps rather than unbroken rings can be easily released to allow detumescence when finished and are obviously safer. Deliberately piercing the penis doesn't cause injury unless the jewelry catches or scratches. Rings and studs have been inserted through the glans and foreskin and the apparently popular "Prince Albert" consists of a ring in through the meatus and out the frenulum or midline on the underside of the penis. Many wearers of this jewelry feel that it heightens sensation and their level of arousal.

As part of man's never-ending search for enhanced stimulation, he has also increased his sense of pelvic fullness by inserting things into his rectum while masturbating. Fingers and dildos with or without vibration ought theoretically to be safe; however, "social injuries of the rectum," as one article referred to them, are potentially lethal. The grease-gun enema that ruptured the bowel, the cement enema that hardened, or the shotgun that went off on insertion are horrible examples of this. A wooden toilet plunger handle has perforated both bowel and bladder, and innumerable pop bottles have lodged beyond the anal sphincter. Photographer Robert Mapplethorpe's bullwhip has artistic effect but traumatic potential. A recent California fad of inserting live insects or animals—such as a shaved gerbil without teeth—is not only cruel to the animal but is also dangerous to the insertee. In addition, no one in the emergency room will believe the story of getting out of the shower to answer the phone, slipping, and falling onto the gerbil. Potential injuries include the previously mentioned lacerations, perforations, infections, and surgical complications. Unless you want to be enshrined forever as a case example in some medical journal, don't put things "up the poop shoot," or "down the chocolate canal." Specially designed "butt plugs" that look like pacifiers can't get lost, and these may be exceptions to that rule.

The most tragic masturbatory fatalities are those associated with autoerotic asphyxiation. The Federal Bureau of Investigation believes that between five hundred and one thousand men accidentally die each year in the United States and Canada because of this.[9] No such feminine fatalities have been reported. A combination of the excitement of risk-taking behavior and cerebral hypoxia (decreased oxygen to the brain) leading to an altered state of consciousness appears to contribute to sexual arousal. Asphyxia is accomplished by hanging, strangulation, or suffocation.[10] Technically, hanging differs from strangulation because of a suspension point. Suffocation includes bags over the head, material stuffed in the mouth, the use of anesthetics or inhalants, and submersion in water. Death occurs when the hypoxia weakens judgment and the victim fails to operate the self-rescue mechanism. Carotid sinus pressure may also lead to loss of consciousness, relaxation, suspension, and asphyxiation.

The literature points out ways to differentiate an autoerotic fatality from suicide; however, that probably offers little consolation to the grieving family, especially if masturbation is thought to be worse than death. In one study, 94 percent of such deaths could be determined to be autoerotic rather than suicide on the basis of "clothing." The autoerotic fatalities were nude, cross-dressed, or the penis was exposed and accessible through an open fly. Other bonds and props such as mirrors and pornography were not associated with suicide. It was not unusual for investigators to find that family members had removed pornography from the death scene.[11]

The FBI has also investigated deaths where electrocution was deliberately used for sexual stimulation as well as when it occurred accidentally with the use of home appliances.

The need for altered states of consciousness by asphyxiation or drugs should be actively discouraged. We need to rediscover natural altered states, such as enhanced orgasm, and stop abusing ourselves.

This is surely an incomplete list of masturbatory techniques, since people have a tremendous creative capacity in the pursuit of pleasure. You who are experimenting with that new technique as you read this: Don't do anything stupid or dangerous!

At this point we should add a few words about nocturnal emissions or "wet dreams." If the erectile mechanism is still a mystery, then the nocturnal emission is an even greater "who done it?" and "how was it done?" There are no statistics as to how often these ejaculations occur, but many men have never experienced one. We shall see later that otherwise sex-negative religious and medical gurus have grudgingly accepted ejaculation while sleeping as more acceptable than deliberate masturbatory ejaculation. "The pressure built up and the dam burst," or "I couldn't help it because I was asleep anyway," produce a state of nonresponsibility that is somehow comforting. There is actually no correlation of emissions with supposed periods of buildup of semen and seminal fluid, and no inverse relationship between the number of nocturnal emissions and the number of other orgasms. Some researchers have found that the number of nocturnal ejaculations is positively correlated with the total number of ejaculations, regardless of modality. Most found no relationship.

We know that erections and vaginal lubrication are a normal part of that stage of sleep that also includes dreaming. The physical "paralysis" at this stage would suggest that unconscious manipulation of the penis is not the mechanism involved in ejaculation. We also know that women can have nocturnal orgasms. They don't stain the sheets, so little attention has been paid to them. It is not inconceivable to assume that heightened arousal during dreaming could produce enough excitement to cross the threshold of orgasm. A study of sexual dream content in people with frequent nocturnal emissions would certainly be helpful in this regard. Regardless of the etiology, nocturnal emission is not included in our definition of masturbation. We're talking about conscious and deliberate self-stimulation.

NOTES

1. William Masters and Virginia Johnson, *Human Sexual Response* (Boston: Little Brown & Co., 1966).

2. Helen Singer Kaplan, *The New Sex Therapy* (New York: Brunner/Mazel, 1974).

3. Shere Hite, *The Hite Report on Male Sexuality* (New York: Knopf, 1981), p. 1106.

4. *Celebrate the Self* 2, no. 1 (1994) p. 7.

5. Hite, *The Hite Report on Male Sexuality*, p. 1106.

6. Shere Hite, *The Hite Report* (New York: Macmillan, 1976), pp. 20ff.

7. Alfred Kinsey, Wardell Pomeroy, and Clyde Martin, *Sexual Behavior in the Human Male* (Philadelphia: W. B. Saunders, 1948).

8. Technical information can be found in the Litten books and in the *Celebrate the Self* newsletter, both of which are available from Factor Press, P.O. Box 8888, Mobile, AL 36689.

9. Robert Hazelwood, Park Dietz, and Ann Burgess, *Autoerotic Fatalities* (New York: St. Martin's Press, 1983).

10. For a first-person account of this phenomenon, see John Money, Gordon Wainright, and David Hinsburger, *The Breathless Orgasm* (Amherst, N.Y.: Prometheus Books, 1991).

11. Alberto Garza-Leal and Francisco Landrón, "Autoerotic Asphyxial Death Initially Misinterpreted as Suicide and a Review of the Literature," *Journal of Forensic Sciences* 36 (1991): 1753–59.

Chapter Four

■

Because It's There

■

Nearly all men and most women masturbate. The phenomenon has been observed during ultrasonic study of male fetuses in utero, in centenarians in nursing homes, and in every age group in between. While it would seem to be an easy task to simply ask people what it is that they do sexually, the gathering of such information is actually quite difficult. This short chapter reflects the shortage of information about masturbatory practices. There have been very few major studies of sexual behavior in the United States.

Historically, sex has not been discussed in polite society. Although there are thousands of individual sex histories in the literature, their focus was on "abnormal" sexuality. Early surveys of "normal" people came out of the social hygiene movement and in attempts to understand sexual physiology.[1] Alfred Kinsey reviewed nineteen American studies done earlier in the twentieth century and found them difficult to generalize.

Kinsey's first study, *Sexual Behavior in the Human Male*, was written with his colleagues at Indiana University in 1948.[2] *Sexual Behavior in the Human Female* followed in

1953.[3] Kinsey did his pioneering work in the 1930s and 1940s and used what is now called a "sample of convenience." That means that he gathered information by means of structured interviews from a self-selected population. In other words, he talked to anyone who would answer his questions. Fifty-three hundred men volunteered. Statistical purists argue that this limited the study's validity because it was biased toward men who were comfortable in talking about sex and who had sexual experiences to discuss. Kinsey found that fifty-one hundred, or 92 percent, of his white, American male population sample had masturbated to orgasm. This broke down statistically as 96 percent for the college educated, 95 percent for the high-school educated, and 87 percent for the grade-school educated. The decreasing frequency of masturbation with decreasing socioeconomic status (less education is a major factor in this) was one of the notable findings in Kinsey's work. This was attributed to lower-class males believing the negative religious and medical warnings about masturbation and to their starting to have sexual intercourse at a younger age. For 68 percent of the men, masturbation was their first ejaculatory experience. For the others it was either intercourse or "wet dreams." In lifetime sexual experiences for the men, masturbation was second in number only to heterosexual intercourse.

Of the twenty-eight hundred women interviewed by Kinsey, 62 percent had masturbated and 58 percent had masturbated to orgasm. Masturbation was the second most frequent sexual activity, after "petting" prior to marriage and second to intercourse after. It was always the most frequently used way to achieve orgasm. The same pattern of educational experience was noted with women as with men. The accumulative index of masturbation at age forty showed that 34 percent of grade-school-educated women had masturbated, but 59 percent of high-school-educated and 63 percent of college-educated women had had that experience.

Fewer than 20 percent of Kinsey's men remembered masturbation before the age of ten. Some of them recalled orgasm. That would certainly be possible given the statistically average age of puberty which Kinsey calculated at thirteen years, seven months. Male puberty appears to be a major organizing factor, as the highest frequency of masturbation was during the early teens, when 88 percent of boys did it with a "minimum average frequency" of twenty-three times per week. The frequency dropped steadily into old age. The lowest reported frequency was once in a lifetime, but nothing more was written about those men at the extremes. Adolescents who masturbated with the highest frequency continued to masturbate with a relatively higher frequency throughout life. Less educated men stopped masturbating earlier than did high-school- and college-educated men, as intercourse became their primary sexual outlet at an earlier age. Masturbation continued to be the chief source of orgasm for college-educated men (and women) until marriage. (So much for those wild college weekends.) During marriage, 69 percent of college-educated men continued to masturbate for 9 percent of their total orgasms. Forty-two percent of high-school-educated and 29 percent of grade-school-educated level men admitted to masturbation in addition to marital intercourse. Kinsey believed that married men masturbated when the wife was absent or had low sex drive; however, he did acknowledge "sexual variety" as a possible motivator. Kinsey also found less masturbation among the "devout" churchgoers at every age and educational level, with the least amount among "devout" Roman Catholics and Orthodox Jews.

Kinsey found more records of masturbatory activity by female infants and young girls than he found for boys. He postulated that girls were more coordinated than boys in rhythmic manual movements. On average, women masturbated less frequently than did men. For unmarried women it was once every two and a half to three weeks and for married women once a month. However, 4 percent reported that at some time in their lives they had masturbated at least fourteen times per week and some reported "ten, twenty, or even one hundred orgasms in an hour." No man could match that. For women, a "devout" religious background was even more a deterrent to masturbation than it was for men.

According to Kinsey, only 28 percent of boys discovered masturbation on their own. Seventy-five percent heard about it and 40 percent observed it. Among women, 70 percent had self-discovered while 43 percent had also heard or read about it. Apparently boys didn't read much. Boys did try it as soon as they learned about it while girls waited until somewhat later. Later survey and anecdotal reports show a higher level of self-discovery in both sexes. The time from beginning masturbation to reaching orgasm was about the same for both sexes—between three and four minutes. Kinsey was the first to note a progressive increase in the incidence of masturbation in younger generations of women and that women with premarital masturbatory experience were more likely to be orgasmic in marital intercourse. He also questioned the distinction between so-called clitoral and vaginal orgasm but he left it to Masters and Johnson to prove that there was no difference. Kinsey was truly a man ahead of his time.

Nineteen seventy-two was a big year for sex. "Fuck" appeared in the dictionary for the first time, the first beaver shot appeared in *Playboy*, and the Playboy Foundation sponsored a study of sexual behavior. They commissioned Research Guild, Inc., to develop a questionnaire to measure the advance of sexual liberalism since the Kinsey survey.

(Yes, this does appear to be a biased perspective.) Public opinion survey teams in twenty-four cities asked people to attend a panel discussion about changes in sexual behavior. Two thousand people, 20 percent of those who had been invited, agreed to attend and then to complete an anonymous questionnaire. Two hundred were interviewed for more information. Morton Hunt collected the results in his book, *Sexual Behavior in the 1970s*.[4] Unfortunately for the statistically minded, the book contains neither the original questionnaire nor the actual data. Age groups were not exactly comparable to Kinsey's, some of the questions were different, and data was sometimes presented in fuzzy numbers, such as "More than one-third agreed." The statistical purists were not happy with Hunt but they probably bought *Playboy* anyway—just to read the stories, of course.

Hunt found that at some point in their lives, 94 percent of his men had masturbated at least once, compared to 92 percent for Kinsey. For women it was 63 percent, compared to Kinsey's 62 percent. Since these numbers were not statistically different from Kinsey's, Hunt had to go beyond them in order to support his theory of increased liberalism. In response to the statement, "Masturbation is wrong," 29 percent of Hunt's men in the over-fifty-five age group agreed, while only 15 percent of the eighteen- to twenty-four-year-old group affirmed that judgment. This finally supported the hypothesis of more liberal attitudes prevailing in the younger group. Sixty-three percent of Hunt's sample had masturbated before age thirteen while only 45 percent of Kinsey's had. The comparable numbers for women were 33 percent and 15 percent, as girls were still not masturbating as early as boys. While Hunt generally found the same trends that Kinsey had found relative to educational level, he did not find the same disparity with regard to religion for males. Ninety-three percent of nonchurchgoers masturbated, as did 92 percent of those who went to church. Women were influenced by church attendance. Seventy-five percent of nonattendees masturbated but only 51 percent of attendees did.

After age thirty, 20 percent of the men in Kinsey's sample had stopped masturbating, and those who continued did so with a frequency of thirty times per year. Hunt found that fewer than 10 percent had stopped and that practitioners were masturbating sixty times per year. For the married men in their twenties and thirties, Kinsey's survey had found that more than 40 percent masturbated with a median frequency of six times per year. Hunt found 72 percent masturbating with a median of twenty-four masturbatory orgasms per year. Hunt did not believe that the increased incidence was correlated with increased heterosexual inadequacy but rather with an increased liberalism in thinking patterns. Hunt found that the same high percentage of men was masturbating as had been twenty-five years earlier, at the time of Kinsey's survey. The differences were that in 1972 they were starting earlier, continuing longer, and masturbating at a higher frequency regardless of marital status.

Hunt postulated that the trend in liberalism would continue as the more permissive attitudes of young parents would be less likely to impose feelings of guilt upon their children. This may be true today as more kids write to newspapers to "ask Beth" and other experts and as they are exposed to more open-minded sex education curricula. Unfortunately, reliable statistics about the present state of attitude evolution are hard to find. The statistical purists have lost the battle to the moral purists. The Study of Health and AIDS Risk Prevalence was designed to quantify the behaviors that place people at risk of HIV infection. The project was awarded to the National Opinion Research Center (NORC) in Chicago and approved by the National Institutes of Health in 1988, but was put on hold by the Bush administration. The American Teenage Study was designed to understand how and why teenagers put themselves at risk of unintended pregnancy and sexually transmitted diseases such as AIDS. The grant was awarded to the University of North Carolina. In 1991 it was cancelled.[5] Both studies fell victim to "family values" and the wholly invalid perception that learning about sexuality promotes sexual experimentation. In reality, sex education promotes responsible sexual behavior. We may have lost a statistical update, but some kids have lost their lives because of this incorrect bias.

The escalating public health issue of AIDS and "at risk" sexual behaviors did ultimately result in updated population sampling. Two studies, one in the United States and one in Britain, were published in 1994, and how they dealt with masturbation is instructive. The NORC in Chicago never received federal funding but did find foundation funding for a probability sample of the general population. The National Health and Social Life Survey was the reincarnation of the Survey of Health and AIDS Risk Prevalence. It was conducted by 220 women who interviewed 3,434 people, aged eighteen to fifty-nine, who lived in households and spoke English. The study reported that "masturbation was generally felt to be the most sensitive topic of any we discussed, making both respondents and interviewers the most uncomfortable." The discomfort was managed by asking only four questions about masturbation; these questions were asked in writing and returned in a sealed envelope. Other topics of similar sensitivity were fantasy, abortion, and personal income. The questions about masturbation covered experience in the last year, orgasm, reasons for masturbation, and associated guilt. Given the different population and the nature of the questions, this study cannot be directly compared to the earlier ones of Kinsey and Hunt. However, of the men in the sample, 63.3 percent reported masturbating in the last year, 26.7 percent at least once a week, 81.5 percent of the time to orgasm, and 54 percent felt guilty about it. For women, the numbers were 41.7 percent masturbating in the last year, 7.6 percent at least once a week, and 61.2 percent to orgasm; however, only 46.8 percent felt guilty about it.[6]

Like its counterpart in the United States, the study of sexual behavior in Britain failed to receive government funding as it had been halted by Margaret Thatcher. It was eventually supported by a private foundation. Questions about masturbation had met with "distaste and embarrassment" during the design phase, so the subject was not part of the interview survey.[7]

It is important to know not only how many people masturbate and why they do so, but also why so many will not participate in surveys. One study of undergraduates who failed to answer questions about masturbation on a sex survey found that these individuals had read fewer books about sexuality and had had fewer sexual partners that did those who did answer the questions.[8] This is not an explanation, but suggests that there are multiple consequences of sexual repression. Another factor is one known in the survey business as "cultural scorn" or "impression management." This is an ingrained sense that a practice (not just masturbation) is shameful and socially undesirable, leading to deliberate nonparticipation and/or nonreporting. Examples of this might include: "I never pick my nose and eat the boogers." "I never spit on the sidewalk." "I never beat off." "Role theory" also suggests that normative expectations of a role dictate the answers to questions. If masturbation is a "guy thing," then women may not acknowledge it. If nurturing and caring are "sissy stuff," then men may deny them.

Despite the apparent shortcomings of "samples of convenience," there is a piece of data that validates their conclusions. A Danish study, which, to the best of my knowledge, has not been published in English (my copy is in German), surveyed a random sample of the entire Danish female population who were seventy, forty, or twenty-two years old in 1980. The age at which masturbation began was progressively earlier and the frequency of masturbation higher for the younger groups.[9] This has been a consistent finding in all surveys regardless of how the sample was obtained. Intuitively this suggests that similar consistent findings are valid as well.

Masturbation isn't supposed to be funny, even though humor often taps into feelings of personal discomfort. How many jerk-off jokes do you know? Actually, there are a few:

The response to both Mr. Bates introducing "my son, Master Bates" and the father asking the driver to let his son, Jack, off at the next corner should be "That's OK with me."

An ad in a local New Zealand butcher shop insists that "Nobody beats Murray's meat."

Why is there a knob at the end of a man's prick? So his hand won't fall off.

> There was a young sailor named Rex
> Who avoided premarital sex
> By thinking of Jesus
> And social diseases
> And beating his meat below decks.

Mother discovered Johnny playing with himself and said, "Stop that or you'll go blind." Johnny replied, "Can I just do it until I need glasses?"

A farmer was cooking stew and let some buckshot fall into the pot. Time was short until supper so he said nothing and served it anyway. The next day his oldest son came to him and said that he had gone to the toilet and then found lead shot in the bowl. The farmer explained and the son was reassured. The second son came with the same complaint and was also reassured. When the youngest son said that he had a problem, the farmer asked if he had found lead in the toilet. "No," replied the son, "I was jerking off in the barn and shot the dog."

The seventy-year-old man went to his physician and asked for something to improve his sex drive because he had a date with a twenty-year-old that night. The doctor hesitated but eventually gave him a pill with a warning to take just half and to be careful. The man returned the next day to report that he had taken the whole pill. "I came twelve times and I'm hurting," he said. "Your back?" inquired the doctor. "No," he replied. "She didn't show up. It's my wrist."

Place one die on your open palm. Does that remind you of a great sexual experience? No? Place a second die on your palm? Does that remind you of a great sexual experience? OK, then close your fist and shake the dice. Does that remind you of a great sexual experience?

Jokes aside, locker room bragging points are for getting laid, not getting off alone: "I came twice with the hair oil, then finished off a third time with the cream." "Way to go, Moe!" High five! Right.

Like women, men will discuss their masturbatory techniques and even their feelings if they are asked properly. In clinical practice, we never ask, "Did you masturbate?" Instead, it's "When did you start masturbating?" Many men are quite willing to discuss masturbation and other aspects of sexuality in depth with surveyors, researchers, and therapists. For these men it may be good to know that they are not alone and to get feedback that their practices are not weird or unique. For many men it also feels good to talk about something that usually feels bad. Sharing feelings of loneliness, discomfort, or inadequacy makes the load a little lighter. It can be the first step toward laying down the burden altogether and finally letting go of the negative feelings and attitudes.

A sense of guilt probably prevents a lot of discussion; however, some men do acknowledge such guilt based on religious notions that masturbation is a sin, unnatural, and morally wrong. After years of religious indoctrination, many a man has reported the words "mortal sin" popping into mind whenever the urge to masturbate occurs. Others base it on medical notions that masturbation causes physical harm, which we will discuss further in chapters 6 and 7. Others recall memories like an examiner in a military recruit depot saying that he could tell if a man were right or left-handed by the way that his penis hung. Prior to 1947, the Naval Academy supposedly rejected potential midshipmen if "on physical examination there is evidence of excessive masturbation."[10] This was probably pretty scary to a south-paw with a cock that listed to port. If he also had pimples, then that was clearly evidence of too much weenie whacking.

Some men do not want to talk about masturbation because they are ashamed. Their image of themselves as "real men" requires that they get their sexual satisfaction exclusively from real women. They certainly should not get satisfaction from other men or from themselves. To admit to masturbation might expose a man as selfish and immature, as unable to attract a partner, as having an inadequate partner, or as being inadequate himself. He might also be seen as unable to control his sexual urges or to express them appropriately. Old associations that "sex is dirty" might be reinforced by having to clean up the ejaculate. It's a wonder then that men are willing to acknowledge masturbation at all. Given all the potential negatives and "scorn," the fact that more than 90 percent of the men who are surveyed acknowledge masturbation appears to accurately reflect the behavior of the population at large.

When we ask men why they manipulate their penises, they give a number of answers. "It feels good." "It's relaxing." "Because it's there." As children and as adults, we learn about our bodies and about our own sexual responses. Recently I heard about a mother who asked her son why he was playing with Willy. "Because Willy likes it," he replied. We learn to identify sensual and sexual feelings and ways to stimulate ourselves. Curiosity and exploration are part of normal development during childhood. As adolescents, we masturbated in response to sexual tension when intercourse was unavailable or unknown. For adults, the reasons are more varied.

Hunt actually asked his sample why they masturbated and he got some interesting answers and results, the fuzzy statistics notwithstanding. Since the numbers add up to more than 100 percent, some of the men were obviously masturbating for multiple reasons. More than 80 percent of the respondents said that they masturbated to relieve sexual tension. (In the more recent Laumann study, 73 percent gave that reason. Forty percent said they did it for pleasure, a choice not given by Hunt.) More than one-third of Hunt's respondents masturbated to relieve "general tension" in order to fall asleep. One-quarter sought comfort when they felt lonely. Many spoke of being able to fantasize various scenarios during masturbation. (See chapter 9 for more about fantasy.) Hunt's young men had many more fantasies than did older men. Older men and the religiously devout were also unlikely to give reasons other than tension reduction (biological drive) for their masturbation. Such tension reduction may be deemed necessary when a man's sex drive is higher than that of his partner, or the partner is temporarily or permanently, psychologically or physically, unavailable. A man may also have no available partner because he is elderly, disabled, and/or single by choice. Masturbation may also serve as voluntary time-out or as a period of "celibacy" for sorting out sexual relationships and considering the directions in which to go. In this era of negotiated mutual consent at each stage of a sexual relationship, it may be easier to masturbate and avoid all those potential boundary violations. Some men consider it a form of meditation or as a path to altered states of consciousness, and therefore a high form of spirituality. As part of an intuitive or prescribed sex therapy program, a man may use masturbation to train himself to achieve and sustain an erection, to delay ejaculation, or to attempt to achieve multiple orgasms. In chapter 11 we will deal with this in much more detail.

Shere Hite asked three thousand women why they masturbated. Hers was also a sample of convenience (questionnaires were distributed via women's movement mailing lists and notices in women's magazines) but, like Hunt, she recorded what sexually active people were actually doing out there in the real world. Eighty-two percent of these women masturbated. The most common reason, again, was relief of sexual tension. Half the women reported masturbating to orgasm after intercourse if they failed to have an orgasm during it. Other reasons given included learning how to have an orgasm, demonstrating independence and self-reliance, and experiencing pure pleasure.[11] At the extreme, some women believe that no man can provide the pleasure that they can provide for themselves. If pregnancy is a goal, then sperm is available elsewhere. A volunteer could produce a sample, or custom sperm from a desired source could be ordered from a sperm bank for artificial insemination. Who needs a relationship with a man?

Even a single masturbatory session may have more than one function, and both positive and negative attitudes may come into play. Masturbation is much more likely to be considered positively if it is experienced as an "alternative" rather than as a "substitute" for "real sex." Besides a feeling of "second best," other barriers to maximum valuation include guilt, worry that sessions are too long or too often, fear of "addiction," and low tolerance for erotic pleasure or for any other inner experience. Masturbation can relieve a sense of loneliness, but it can also intensify that feeling. Any behavior may cause disappointment by failing to achieve its goal, and masturbation is no exception to this. Unrealistic expectations can set up negative feelings.

Masturbation is private, provides an easy, intense physical pleasure, and provides immediate feedback. It could be an unending source of good feelings.

Certainly not all reasons for masturbation are positive. Some may masturbate just because it is "bad" or "naughty" and they want to challenge the "rules." Some may masturbate compulsively or "addictively" and be out of control. Some may wish to avoid intimacy with a partner or to avoid sex with another person for illogical or even psychotic reasons, such as a fear that teeth in the vagina might bite off a penis. Some may be withdrawing from and/or punishing a partner, reassuring themselves when they feel rejected, or avoiding what they perceive as dependency on another person. In these cases, masturbation may result in loss of relationship, overwhelming guilt or shame, or a need to act out sexually against others. Obviously, these are not value-free acts and, in these cases, masturbation may serve to avoid dealing with issues that would be better addressed in therapy.

A number of these reasons apply to each of us. One of the tasks of midlife review is to identify the origins of our feelings, especially those of guilt and shame. The next several chapters should help us in doing that.

NOTES

1. Vern Bullough, *Science in the Bedroom* (New York: Basic Books, 1994).

2. Alfred Kinsey, Wardell Pomeroy, and Clyde Martin, *Sexual Behavior in the Human Male* (Philadelphia: W. B. Saunders, 1948), esp. chap. 14.

3. Alfred Kinsey, Wardell Pomeroy, Clyde Martin, et al., *Sexual Behavior in the Human Female* (Philadelphia: W. B. Saunders, 1953), esp. chap. 5. Most of the following statistical comparisons between men and women are summarized in a chart on pp. 173–75.

4. Morton Hunt, *Sexual Behavior in the 1970s* (Chicago: Playboy Press, 1974), esp. chap. 2.

5. Howard Ruppell, in *Newsletter of the Society for the Scientific Study of Sexuality* (March 1992).

6. Edward Laumann, John Gagnon, Robert Michael, et al., *The Social Organization of Sexuality* (Chicago: University of Chicago Press, 1994), pp. 80–86.

7. Kaye Wellings, Julia Field, Anne Johnson, et al., *Sexual Behaviour in Britain* (London: Penguin, 1994).

8. Joseph Catania, Lois McDermott, and Lance Pollack, "Questionnaire Response Bias and Face-to-Face Interview Sample Bias in Sexuality Research," *Journal of Sex Research* 22 (1986): 52–72.

9. Eva Fog, J. Lunde, K. Garde, et al., "Sexualverhalten, erfahrungen, wissen und einstellungen Dänisher frauen," in *Praktische Sexual Medizine*, ed. Wolf Eicher (Wiesbaden: Verlag Medical Tribune GmbH, 1987).

10. Kinsey, Pomeroy, and Martin, *Sexual Behavior in the Human Male*, p. 513.

11. Shere Hite, *The Hite Report* (New York: Macmillan, 1976), pp. 14, 435.

Chapter Five

Other Critters and Cultures Take Things in Hand

Surveys tell us that humans do it. Observations reveal that monkeys and many other mammals do it. Masturbation is part of our animal heritage. It is, however, a rather late development in the evolution of sexuality. The simplest animals such as yeasts and sponges reproduce asexually (literally, "without sex") by cell division, budding, or cloning. The simplest "sexual" species such as fish and amphibians practice external fertilization by depositing eggs and sperm in the ocean and hoping for the best. More complex animals must create an internal "ocean" surrounded by a calcified shell or uterus and, consequently, the male needs a tool for internal fertilization. In the evolutionary sequence, the first group of animals with a penis-like organ was the reptiles. While reptiles, insects, and birds do possess a penis of sorts, there is no literature to suggest that they engage in self-stimulation or, for that matter, any other nonreproductive sexual activity. In explanation, these animals are seasonal breeders and the influence of light on the pineal gland, mating sounds, pheromones (sex stimulating scents), combinations of these, and possibly other factors trigger testosterone secretion in the male and induce procreative activity.

There is no evidence of recreational sex in submammalian species. There are anecdotes that birds such as parrots and parakeets may mimic human thrusting behavior as well as the human voice, but there is no good evidence that they are masturbating for self-stimulation. A woman at a cocktail party once told me about a parakeet who humped her finger ("Aeneas the green one, not Achilles the blue one"). It's amazing what people will tell you when they know your research interests.

Lower mammals are locked into estrus cycles where female receptivity is signaled by pheromones which trigger male arousal and procreative performance. Witness the neighborhood cats and dogs when a cat or bitch is in heat. As we shall see, it is only in the most highly evolved mammals, the primates, that sex is not seasonal and can have many nonprocreative purposes, including social bonding, tension release, bartering, and pleasure.

There isn't much in the scientific literature, or any other literature for that matter, about animal sexuality in general or animal masturbation in particular. The pioneers in the ethological (cross-species) and ethnological (cross-cultural) study of sex were Yale anthropologists Clellan Ford and Frank Beach. In their 1951 book *Patterns of Sexual Behavior*, they reviewed the literature and presented data about the sexual activities—including masturbation—of mammals from mice to men.[1] This is still the definitive work on the subject. Mark Walters's 1988 book about animal courtship has only one reference to masturbation, the same 1937 observations of English red deer by Frank Fraser Darling as had been previously noted by Ford and Beach.[2] A computer search of the world's literature for the last thirty years yielded two further references in English. A time budget study of nine dairy bulls in a semen production center showed that they spent one-tenth of 1 percent of their time masturbating, sometimes to orgasm. Their daily activity was recorded by camera. Each bull masturbated at 5 A.M. and 4 P.M. The handlers worked from 5:30 A.M. to 3:30 P.M.[3] In the second reference, veterinarians injected breeding horses with imipramine (a human antidepressant) in order to increase their sexual productivity. If no mares were present after they received the medication, the stallions reliably got erections and masturbated by bouncing the erect penis against the belly. Some ejaculated.[4] In both studies, it was noted that masturbation is common in stallions and bulls in stalls, in fields, and in the wild.

Ford and Beach observed that animals examine, groom, touch, and manipulate their sexual organs. Only the most biased, antisexual observer could argue that such cleaning accompanied by pelvic thrusting was never experienced as pleasurable. It was once thought that self-stimulation was characteristic only of hormone-driven caged or captive animals without access to other animals. This does occur and observers probably identify with the "frustration"; however, field studies have shown that some animals in the wild do stimulate themselves. Male rodents may sit up and stimulate their genitals with forepaws or mouths. Some animals employ inanimate objects as sources of genital stimulation. One male porcupine was observed to straddle a stick and bump it along the ground; however, porcupines are more commonly observed to rub the penis itself vigorously along the ground. Many of us have experienced a dog thrusting against our leg or watched as Handsome Dan, the Yale bulldog, humped the cheerleader's megaphone at halftime.

Masturbatory details are quite limited in the published descriptions of animal sexual behavior. A male elephant may manipulate his penis with his trunk. Dolphins have no appendages with which to touch themselves but captive males have been seen to hold an erect penis in a jet of water or to rub it against the floor of the tank. During rutting season, red deer stags collect a harem of hinds (does). Darling observed the stags to frequently mount the does as expected, but he also observed them to draw their sensitive new antlers through the brush and along the ground. This was followed by erection and ejaculation without thrusting. Such "masturbation" occurred several times per day.[5] Among subprimate mammals, then, deer, horses, and bulls have been observed to masturbate to orgasm, as have ponies, goats, sheep, camels, ferrets, porcupines, elephants, rabbits, dogs, rats, cats, chinchillas, skunks, raccoons, and guinea pigs.

Is masturbation in conflict with the principle of Darwinian selective advantage? While intuitively we may sense that masturbation is normal and natural, we have previously lacked a rational response to the argument that sperm on the ground, sheets, hands, or tissues are not in a proper position to fertilize eggs and continue the species, and are therefore in an unnatural place.

In *Sperm Wars* Robin Baker, an evolutionary biologist brought light to this seeming contradiction to Darwinian thinking.[6] Evolutionary biologists see sexual behavior in terms of the survival of the fittest members of any species where males are in competition with each other to fertilize the available females. Social or sexual monogamy is biologically irrelevant to the process of having the fittest sperm in the neighborhood. Not all sperm are the same. The average thirty-year-old man produces three hundred million sperm each day. Fewer than 10 percent of these are "egg-getters" and the potency of these is short-lived. Sperm are produced in the testes and line up in the vas deferens, like in the old Woody Allen movie *Everything You Always Wanted to Know about Sex But were Afraid to Ask*, as they await ejaculation. The oldest and least active are at the head of the line. These geriatric sperm up front have to make way for the younger, more dynamic sperm who have a higher probability of beating out the competition to fertilize an egg. Frequent ejaculation maintains the supply of younger, more energetic sperm to biological advantage. Even if some old-timers are released by frequent intercourse, frequent masturbation would make it even more likely that the active youngsters will be at the head of the line and more likely to fertilize an available egg. So masturbation promotes survival of the fittest.

Continuing a military analogy, there is a tactical advantage for a man to keep his sperm in peak fighting condition for the "wars" while keeping the competition from doing the same. He masturbates in secret while trying to shame the competition out of topping up with active sperm so that they are not as prepared as he is. Hypocrisy is essential to the maintenance of reproductive success, hence the universal condemnation of a universal practice. The process is biological, but the rationalization is social, and humankind has been wonderfully adept at rationalizing this particular instinctive behavior.

Lower animals don't have to rationalize what they do instinctively. The dominant male is the most sexually active. Potency is maintained by frequent ejaculations which may include masturbation. High sexual tension might also be secondary to high testosterone levels that also promote fighting with other males for dominance. It might be a response to the pheromones in the air. It might just be pleasurable. "The pursuit of sexual pleasure is . . . an elaborate device ensuring maintenance of the genetic system in the mammalian prelude to reproduction," wrote Lynn Margulis and Dorion Sagan in *Origins of Sex*.[7] Masturbation, per se, obviously doesn't reproduce the fittest animals, but it is crucial to the active sexuality of the dominant animals. It wasn't coincidence that the masturbating bulls were working in a semen production center or that the masturbating horses were at stud. In the world of animals, masturbation appears to be just a healthy sign of active sexuality. Survey data suggest that this is true for human animals as well.

The biological task of males is to scatter their plentiful sperm as widely as possible. Females nurture the precious egg, find a suitable sperm donor, and rear the offspring. For the male to disseminate his sperm, orgasm and ejaculation are required. For females, orgasm is not necessary for ovulation. I am aware of no documentation of subprimate female "orgasm." From a behavioral perspective, there is little pleasurable, positive reinforcement in the process of impregnation and birth. The guys have all the fun. In many species, females are sexually receptive only during the "heat" of estrus cycles. Males could, in theory at least, be "aroused" constantly by a series of females. In most species, males play little or no role in parenting and are free to do other things. Mothers don't have time for recreational sex. It should come as no surprise then that subprimate females engage in less sexual activity than do males. This includes masturbation. This does not provide a biological explanation for female orgasm. There is no evidence that orgasm helps propel sperm up to the egg. The pleasure of orgasm probably does not positively reinforce having intercourse because the frequency of orgasm during intercourse is so low. The biology may simply that in the clitoris is analogous to the erectile penis where spasm is necessary for ejaculation; muscle spasm becomes the peak response for females as well.

Nonprocreational sexual activity is observed most frequently among the primates, including monkeys, apes, and humans. This parallels the development of the opposable thumb as well as the development of abstract intelligence and symbolic thought. The former adds options for self-stimulation. The latter reaches its highest level in human fantasy. The concept of symbolism (one thing standing for another) is vital to the understanding of evolving sexuality. I recall from readings in introductory psychology an experiment in symbolism in which chimpanzees were rewarded with poker chips for some task, such as pulling levers (a psychologist's favorite). Since the chimps could then trade the chips for bananas and apples, the poker chips became symbols for food. It didn't take the female chimps long to discover that they could do their nails while the males pulled the levers, earned the chips, and then traded the chips for sex. The females then used the chips to get the bananas and apples. It was clear that the chimps understood symbolism. It is tempting to assume that some chimps might stimulate themselves sexually while thinking about food, poker chips, or their last sexual encounter with another chimp. We'll probably never know for sure, but we do know that such associations do exist for humans.

Observers of primate colonies, both in captivity and in the wild, witness a great deal of sexual activity apart from males mounting females. Monkeys and apes appear to masturbate for the pleasure it provides. Ford and Beach included field observation of a spider monkey manipulating his penis with the tip of his prehensile tail and of rhesus monkeys and baboons masturbating. Female monkeys were observed to masturbate much less frequently and without the dramatic climax seen in males. Male great apes will masturbate with hand, mouth, foot, and combinations thereof. Walters described a great deal of nonprocreative sex play among bonobos, the animals previously known as pygmy chimpanzees. This included bartering sex for food, face-to-face copulation, female-female genital contact, and male-infant sex play.[8] Ford and Beach quoted Bingham's 1928 observations of female chimpanzee masturbatory activity which, while less active than male activity, included rubbing the vulva against the bars of the cage as well as against boxes, pool balls, and mangoes. One chimp inserted a large leaf into her vagina and then bounced the leaf against the bars of the cage, thereby inventing a vibrator.[9]

Obviously, the great apes demonstrate experimental, symbolic sexual activity similar to that seen in humans. We assume that it serves the same function.

In moving from the ethological to the ethnological comparisons, Ford and Beach made the statement that "at least a few members of every society do indulge in masturbatory practices."[10] Unfortunately, that knowledge was limited in 1951 and it is still limited today. Ford and Beach gathered their facts from the forerunner of what is now known as the Human Relations Area Files. These are housed in an old mansion in New Haven, Connecticut, but they now are also available on microfiche, CD-ROM, and online at subscribing colleges and universities. The files contain over a million pages of information about 360 societies from over sixty-three hundred sources. The researcher using the paper or microfiche files to study masturbation would start with codes 839 for Sexual Behavior and 864 for Sex Education. For each of the 335 societies there, that code's file space contains copies of marginally noted pages from the source documents. By reading the annotated material for these two codes, the researcher then finds references to masturbation. I could find only twenty-eight of these files that had such information. Data have been entered exclusively online since 1993, and a search there under "masturbation" yields an additional thirteen references, for a total of forty-one societies, past and present, with a documented practice of masturbation. For the other three hundred plus societies, the data were never collected. Even if it were recorded, the information was not uniformly gathered by anthropologists intent on producing an accurate and unbiased description of the native culture. Missionaries, explorers, and other untrained observers may have left the only records of some societies prior to their "civilization" by Westerners. These observers were obviously products of their own Western cultures and showed the attendant biases in data collection.

Some of the bias was obvious. "The young heathen . . . do not practice two vices which are prevalent amongst certain civilized nations, onanism and sodomy. These immoral customs were entirely unknown in the Thonga tribe before the coming of civilisation. . . . The natives themselves do not consider this sin as of any importance at all."[11] Or, in explaining the "dullness" that keeps the Fellahin a backward race, "Some sociologists put it down to masturbation which is fairly common in the Islamic East; but this vice seems limited to cities, for the country people are much less morbid."[12] "Long before puberty, they [the Rundi of Africa] are enlightened about sexual matters and have learned many loathsome things of a sexual nature from those who are older. This does not mean that they have sexual intercourse at a very early age, but onanism and masturbation are widespread vices."[13]

Edward Hunt noted that among the Yaps of Oceania, "Self-abuse is already begun in their fifth to sixth years and becomes more frequent with age. Aided by sexual play among children, it may hinder the development of normal sexual feelings. The frequent masturbation of the females may lead to the diminution of physiological sense in normal intercourse and result at least in cold-heartedness."[14]

The absence of reports is not necessarily reliable either. When a researcher writes, "This vice seems never to have been practiced by the Nkundo,"[15] one wonders what question he asked. M. C. Goswami and D. N. Majumda asked adolescents in an Indian village if they masturbated and were told that the practice was unknown. They then cited another field researcher, T. Sanha, who had observed the practice at "addictive levels" in the same village. Interestingly, they thought that Sanha was biased and so discounted his observations.[16] Individuals in other societies may have felt enough shame about masturbation that they denied its occurrence or were unwilling to talk about it. One must be especially skeptical about languages that supposedly have "no word for *masturbation*." The word search questions would have to be especially clear, sensitive, and unbiased in order to elicit such words as "make semen boil over" or "pierce the vagina with her hand" (Trobrianders), or "game with tree that shakes" or "vagina sport" (Gondi).

We also need to look beyond the words. Among the Tikopia, "masturbation seems to be a very frequent practice among the young people of both sexes. It is regarded by the natives as being due to the absence of sexual intercourse, not to inversion. 'When a young man dwells and has no sweetheart, then he rubs his member. He is called *tae viri* (filth rubber).' . . . The principal objection to the practice is alleged to be that it is unpleasant for the hands after having been thus occupied to turn to the preparation of food."[17] This very common practice, then, is seen not with moral condemnation but in the same light as that restroom notice that admonishes: "Employees must wash their hands before returning to the kitchen."

Despite the bias in reporting, a pattern does emerge in known cross-cultural responses to masturbation. The practice is generally approved or tolerated in infants and young children, tolerated or mildly condemned in adolescents, and ridiculed or condemned in adults except when the circumstances are noncompetitive. This represents the progressive imposition of societally approved standards on naturally occurring behaviors, especially when that behavior in post-pubescent males might challenge the generative capability of the older adults. Like other instinctive responses, the condemnation is unconscious and subject to conscious rationalization.

For infants and children, masturbation is often acknowledged as a normal and natural part of self-discovery and rehearsal for adult sexuality. While young animals often play at mounting, this behavior is not generally accepted in human cultures. The data are limited, but societies that tolerate such childhood sex play also seem to tolerate or even encourage masturbation. "The adult persons [Manchu] pet small children. The mothers suck their small boys' penis and tickle the sexual parts of girls."[18] Fondling the infant son's penis was also noted among the Kpeppe of Liberia, the Thai, and the Siriono of South America. Among the latter, "Children, especially boys, finger their genitals a great deal without censure, and when they are young, their parents masturbate them frequently."[19] Among the Lepcha of the Himalayas, children's play is often sexual. There is both boy-girl and boy-boy simulated intercourse. The boys tie their penises together. "Adults think sex play funny yet childish; far from disapproving, they are more likely to egg them on."[20] "When boys [Teluga of India] are seen manipulating their organs, the elders guide and playfully remove their hands from them. Boys invariably start doing so again, and are not admonished."[21] Among the Pilaga of Argentina, young children are permitted significant sexual freedom. "Up to age 5 boys masturbate and practice pederasty [anal intercourse] unashamedly in broad daylight. The girls masturbate against one another in public, and at five years they start taking little boys to bed and practicing coitus. Open masturbation by rubbing against other children, games of snatching at genitalia, and open "coitus bees" in which groups of little boys and girls attempt coitus at night, continue until about the age of 12."[13]

Among the Tarahumara of Mexico, "masturbation by boys was acknowledged by all informants. No particular sentiment against this practice was voiced. There is a joking attitude taken toward it and it is not considered harmful."[23] Fort the Aymara of Peru, "the sex play of young children is viewed by adults with tolerant amusement, and masturbation, although ridiculed, is not actively disapproved, with the results that informants recall having practiced it with no apparent feelings of shame or guilt."[24] Among the Marquesas "if the child becomes too troublesome, an adult might quiet it by masturbating it. The masturbation of female children began very early; in fact, from the moment of birth there was systematic manipulation of the labia to elongate them, as elongation was considered a mark of beauty."[25]

Shame rather than guilt was characteristic of the societies studied by Margaret Mead. In *Coming of Age in Samoa* Mead noted, "Masturbation is an all but universal habit, beginning at the age of 6 or 7. . . . Boys masturbate in groups but among little girls it is a more individualistic, secretive practice. This habit seems never to be a matter of individual discovery, one child always learns from another. The adult ban only covers the unseemliness of open indulgence. The adult attitude towards all the details of sex is characterized by the view that they are unseemly, not that they are wrong."[26]

Similarly, among the Manus of *Growing Up in New Guinea*, Mead reported that sexual behaviors other than heterosexual activity "are enveloped in the prevailing atmosphere of shame, but escape the stigma of sin. Masturbation is practiced by the children but always in solitude and solitude is hard to find. It seems to have no important psychological concomitants; engendering as it does no very special shame in a society where every act of excretion is lamentable and to be most carefully hidden."[27] Shame is also characteristic of Marquesas where boys often masturbate in groups with penis and hand moistened with saliva to see who can ejaculate first; however, it would be shameful if this were to be witnessed by adults.[28] Again in Oceania, the Trobrianders "regarded [masturbation] as undignified but in a rather amused and entirely indulgent manner."[29]

There are negative cultures. In Tibet,

sexual games between children, as well as masturbation, were very severely punished if discovered by parents. The father would beat a child caught playing with itself or attempting coitus with another child. Mothers, it seems, did not beat, but pinched instead, and this could be made very unpleasant for the victim.

In very small children, masturbation was repressed by attempts to frighten the child. It would be told by its mother that a sort of witch called a baghzi would come and either carry the child away, or cut off its ears and put them in a leather bag which the creature carried expressly for the purpose of collecting the ears of bad children. No threat was ever made that the genital organs of the child would be cut off, and the idea that this might be said seemed utterly fantastic to my informants.[30]

John Honigman wrote that the Eskimos of Upper Kaska believed that masturbation led to insanity and blindness and it was punished by whipping the child's hands with a willow switch.[31] Among the Kurds, "some parents beat their children for this, and others advise them."[32]

In Taiwan, "if a child is discovered masturbating, he is severely scolded and beaten. He is threatened with what will happen if he continues; he will be unable to urinate or he will go crazy."[33] Among the Kogi in Colombia, "Castration is . . . the threat used to prohibit masturbation. Masturbatory manipulations by male children are regarded as a serious danger to the sexuality of the father and, it is said, lead to the End of the World. The same is said with reference to girls, but in this case it does not affect the parents magically, but rather the health of the girl herself. Masturbation is thus regarded as 'very bad.' "[34] Paradoxically, Gerado Reichel-Dolmatoff noted that mothers may masturbate young children to calm them and make them sleep. They obviously don't tell the fathers. The author also noted that masturbation was common among adult women.

Acceptable adolescent sex play is culturally determined.

When heterosexual sex play is discouraged, masturbation is more likely to occur. In cultures that have a defined initiation or rite of passage to adulthood, the practice of masturbation is supposed to be left behind at that time. The more authoritarian and controlling the society, the more masturbation is punished. For the previously permissive Teluga, masturbation is more stealthily practiced and elders are no longer indulgent. Ridicule and threat are employed to cure the habit: "If you persist in this habit, your organ will not grow," or "it will become crooked and you will be useless." Older boys seem to know that this is not true and they continue to masturbate secretly, occasionally jointly or mutually.[35] Jomo Kenyatta, writing about the Kikuyu of Kenya in 1938, indicated that "before initiation it is considered right and proper for boys to practice masturbation as a preparation for their future sexual activities. Sometimes two or more boys compete in this to see which can show himself more active than the rest. This practice takes place outside the homestead, under a tree or bush, where the boys are not visible to their elders. It is considered an indecency to be seen doing it, except by boys of the same age-grade. The practice is given up after the initiation ceremony and anyone seen doing it after that would be looked upon as clinging to a babyish habit and be laughed at, because owing to the free sex-play which is permitted among young people, there is no need to indulge in it." The "free sex-play" however, is Ngweko, a mutual masturbation by girls and boys (other than blood relatives) wherein the girl keeps her skirt tight and the couple rub together without touch or penetration. "Masturbation among girls is considered wrong, and if a girl is seen by her mother even so much as touching that part of her body, she is at once told that she is doing wrong. It may be said that this, among other reasons, is probably the motive of trimming the clitoris, to prevent girls from developing sexual feelings around that point."[36] These girls need to be virgins at the time of marriage in order to command the best bride price.

Among the Lepcha of the Himalayas, adolescent masturbation "is seldom indulged in by reason of the fact that women are available from the earliest moment that a boy feels the need of sex. The general feeling is that it is slightly silly and rather funny."[39] On the other hand, when there is a taboo against intercourse, "we feel lonely and dissatisfied so we catch hold of the tree which shakes and milk it like a cow till the seeds come out. This is our pleasure."[38] Similarly among the Tikopia of Oceania, masturbation among adolescents is regarded as normal in the absence of heterosexual intercourse.[39] Honigman made the same observation among Nahane Eskimos.

There is little cross-cultural data about adult masturbation. Colin Turnbull did note that among the Mbuti of Africa, *ai ofuni* happens. "I have met several [men] who talk, with great poetry, of the joys of masturbating when alone in the moonlight"[40] Among one group of Australian aborigines "the preliminary to every totemic ceremony is [group] masturbation."[41] In Africa, the Azande women "often resort to mutual masturbation using bananas or manioc, sweet potato roots shaped with a knife into a phallus, for the purpose."[42]

On Truk, "for those forbidden intercourse by ritually prescribed continence or unable to find a sexual partner, masturbation carries no stigma for either men or women. For a man this is not done in an exhibitionist manner . . . in the company of other men masturbation requires no more discretion than, for example, urination: he draws apart and turns his back. Women also masturbate alone by stimulating the clitoris."[43] Raymond Firth also saw autoeroticism in terms of social utility, not morality. "It is said that only women who have already tasted sexual pleasure will act thus. Such a woman 'remembers the male organ' and with her finger, or a manioc root, or a peeled banana, rubs herself. She does so with increasing energy as her desire climbs up. It is because of the force used that it is customary to peel the banana; otherwise her genitals would become sore."[44]

Statistical studies in the United States by Kinsey and Hunt stand alone; however, Kinsey had noted that Western European statistics were similar to his own. Two recent international studies of university students (arguably adults) are of interest in this regard. In Colombia, 95 percent of men and 68 percent of women had masturbated, numbers remarkably similar to those in the United States. We know that this is a different culture, however, because 51 percent of the men had also had sex with a prostitute. That was down from 92 percent in a study done twenty years earlier.[45] In China, only 77 percent of men and 29 percent of women had masturbated by age twenty-two. Fewer than 5 percent of either group had had sexual intercourse. Fifty percent of the group thought that masturbation was harmful to health, and 83 percent thought it caused "frigidity."[46] Hong Kong Chinese men and women living in Canada also had lower masturbation frequencies, more similar to Far Eastern Chinese than to European Canadians.

The Confucian heritage makes China different from other Far Eastern countries where the frequency of masturbation is similar to that in the West. In one 1995 survey, 98 percent of Japanese men masturbated and 80 percent also reported wet dreams. Japanese women were not surveyed.[47] Ninety-five percent of male Thai medical students masturbated, as did 33 percent of the women. Eighteen percent of the men visited prostitutes, down from the 49 percent who had done so ten years earlier.[48] The dangers of sexually transmitted diseases are known throughout the world, even to doctors.

The 1997 *International Encyclopedia of Sexuality* included reports on thirty-two countries "each by a scholar familiar with a particular country and its culture." Each report has a section entitled "Autoerotic Behaviors and Patterns"; however, most or these are only a paragraph or two in length and limited to survey data about the frequency of masturbation. All are consistent with what has already been noted, but a few additional points are of interest. Eighty-seven percent of Australian women reported a history of masturbation, the highest frequency in the Western world. This was attributed to "a more relaxed attitude about sexual behaviour." From the Muslim world, girls in Bahrain are taught to wash their genitals "with finger and thumb closed" in order to avoid reaching and feeling. In Iran the only reference to self-pleasuring "appears to be within the context of pre-prayer ablutions requirements on the male after voluntary ejaculation." From the Ukraine, attitudes "reflect the [former] Soviet view that sex is shameful and not a useful human activity for the socialist society." Finally, one Japanese survey that did include women found only 30 percent to have masturbated: "A good Japanese woman should always be modest in any sexual activity."[49]

The sex negativity of some Eastern cultures is reflected in the so-called culture-bound syndromes recognized in the medical literature. An ancient treatise of Indian medicine, the *Charak Samhita*, defined semen as the elixir of life. Forty meals produced one drop of blood; forty drops of blood, one drop of bone marrow; and forty drops of bone marrow, one drop of semen. By working out the math, that comes to one ejaculation in a lifetime, fewer for those who habitually skip breakfast. Each ejaculation is therefore precious and causes a tremendous loss of energy in terms of power and longevity. Any loss of semen would be life-threatening. Given that high level of anxiety, it is not surprising that a generalized anxiety syndrome, including vague physical symptoms and weakness, would be attributed to excessive semen loss. Masturbation, nocturnal emissions, premarital intercourse, extramarital intercourse, and excessive marital intercourse all lead to guilt and a culturally accepted cluster of anxiety-related symptoms known as *dhat* on the Indian subcontinent and as *shenkui* in China. Another syndrome, *koro*, is common among Chinese. This period of sudden and intense anxiety that the penis will retract and disappear into the body, causing sudden death, is also attributed to excessive loss of semen. One Indian source described epidemics of *koro*, a mass hysteria of disappearing dicks.[50] All that anxiety about semen loss would clearly suggest that masturbation is not acceptable in that cultural context.

There is some interesting data about black sexuality in the United States. In one study of college students, black men masturbated less frequently than did white (56 percent to 81 percent) and were more likely to have had intercourse (95 percent to 80 percent). Similarly, black females masturbated less frequently than white females (48 percent to 66 percent) and were also more likely to have had intercourse (90 percent to 80 percent).[51] In another study, both black men and black women had lower rates of masturbation and nocturnal orgasms and higher rates of heavy petting and intercourse. They also had intercourse earlier than did their white counterparts.[52] Kinsey and Edward Laumann had previously found the same pattern in both men and women. The latter noted that 40 percent of black males currently masturbated and 67 percent had had lifetime experience. Forty-three percent of black women currently masturbated and lifetime experience was 63 percent. These studies suggested that the different rates were a function of race and not of social class.[53]

Several theories address such cultural differences in the expression of sexuality. "Sexual scripting" suggests that patterns of sexual conduct in a culture are socially determined.[54] The meaning of a particular sexual behavior, such as masturbation or having a mistress, would be transmitted to the individual by the social responses to it and the cultural script would be retained. Individuals might make minor adaptations to suit their own needs and if enough individuals improvised upon and changed cultural scenarios, then the culture itself would change. The "social constructionist" perspective on sexual behavior finds its origin to be in the sociohistorical process and its legitimacy derived from cultural practices of the time and place. Attitudes toward homosexuality and prostitution are examples of this. Behaviors once considered to simply be evolved drives associated with species survival take on differing cultural values. They evolve as a society evolves and they clearly have the potential to change.[55]

James Hillman, a Jungian analyst, has followed up on Carl Jung's argument that societal prohibition works only because it echoes a collective, instinctual, self-regulating inhibition. This must be true for masturbation because, despite all the intellectual evidence to the contrary, the fundamental guilt about masturbation seems unresolvable. Hillman argues that this is so because after adolescence inhibition is an integral part of masturbation itself.[56] This is consistent with the evolutionary, instinctive, biological explanation that "sperm wars" are part of the human psyche.

If our shared animal task is to beget little starfish, porcupines, bulldogs, chimps, or humans, then does the spider monkey with his tail wrapped pleasurably around his penis realize that he is failing in his procreative duty? Does the stallion bouncing his penis against his belly understand that he is failing to preserve his sperm for insemination? Does the red deer rubbing his new antlers against the ground and ejaculating realize that he should be impregnating the does? Obviously not. But does the human with the opposable thumb wrapped around his penis believe that he should instead be having intercourse or conserving his sexual energy? You bet he does.

From birth onward, every human child in every society is taught about sex, and the lessons, explicit or implicit, are different. Human symbolism can work positively or negatively. Masturbation may be associated with the pleasure of sensual touching or with intimacy or power or tension release, or it may be associated with shame or guilt. Each culture has rules. Children learn that sexual activity is playful or sinful, permissible or forbidden, guilt-ridden, shameful, silly, fun, or joyful. Certain activities are acceptable, others are not. Some are possible for one age group but not for another. Adults have been conditioned to different opinions about what is normal, moral, or natural. There is no absolute truth, only that which one learns in a particular cultural context.

We ought to be able to see now how we have been conditioned in our attitudes by the society in which we grew up. Similar patterns in "social constructionism" will emerge as we look at religious, medical, and educational contributions to our feelings about masturbation. For us, the important message is that such attitudes evolve and are therefore subject to change.

Notes

1. Clellan Ford and Frank Beach, *Patterns of Sexual Behavior* (New York: Harper and Row, 1951).

2. Mark Walters, *The Dance of Life: Courtship in the Animal Kingdom* (New York: Arbor House, 1988).

3. Katherine Houpt and Gwendolyn Wollney, "Frequency of Masturbation and Time Budgets of Dairy Bulls Used for Semen Production," *Applied Animal Behaviour Science* 24 (1989): 217–25.

4. S. M. McDonnell et al., "Imipramine-Induced Erection, Masturbation, and Ejaculation in Male Horses," *Pharmacology, Biochemistry & Behavior* 27(1987): 187–91.

5. Ford and Beach, *Patterns of Sexual Behavior*, p. 161.

6. Robin Baker, *Sperm Wars: The Science of Sex* (New York: Basic Books, 1996).

7. Lynn Margulis and Dorion Sagan, *Origins of Sex* (New Haven: Yale University Press, 1986).

8. Walters, *Dance of Life*, p. 157.

9. Ford and Beach, *Patterns of Sexual Behavior*, p. 162.

10. Ibid., p. 165.

11. Henri Junod, *The Life of a South African Tribe* (London: Macmillan & Co., 1927), p. 98.

12. Hamed Ammar, *Growing Up in an Egyptian Village: Silwa, Province of Aswan* (London: Routledge & Kegan Paul, 1954), p. 192.

13. Hans Meyer, *Die Barundi* (Leipzig: O H Spamer, 1916), p. 173.

14. Edward Hunt, David Schneider, Nathaniel Kidder, et al., *The Micronesians of Yap and Their Depopulation* (Washington, D.C.: National Research Council, 1949), p. 164.

15. Gustave Hulstaert, *Marriage among the Nkundu* (Brussells: VanCampenhout, 1938), p. 97.

16. M. C. Goswami and D. N. Majumda, "A Study of the Social Attitudes among the Garo." (New Haven, Conn.: Human Relations Area Files [computer file], 1998).

17. Raymond Firth, *We the Tikopia: A Sociological Study of Kinship in Primitive Polynesia* (London: Gage, Allen & Unwin Ltd., 1936), p. 494.

18. S. M. Shirokogoroff, *Social Organization of the Manchus* (Shanghai: Royal Asiatic Society, 1924), p. 122.

19. Allen Holmberg, "The Siriono: A Study of the Effect of Hunger Frustration on the Culture of a Semi-Nomadic Bolivian Indian Tribe" (Ph.D. diss., Yale University, 1946), p. 189.

20. Geoffrey Gorer, *Himalayan Village: An Account of the Lepchas of Sikkim* (London: Michael Joseph Ltd., 1938), p. 310.

21. S. C. Dube, *Indian Village* (Ithaca: Cornell University Press, 1955), p. 193.

22. Henry Jules and Zunia Henry, *Doll Play of Pilaga Indian Children* (New York: Vintage Books, 1974), p. 32.

23. Jacob Fried, "Ideal Norms and Social Control in Tarahumara Society" (Ph.D. diss., Yale University, 1951), p. 150.

24. Harry Tschopik, "The Aymara of Chucuito, Peru," *Anthropological Papers of the American Museum of Natural History* 44 (1951): 167.

25. Ralph Linton, "Marquesan Culture," in *The Individual and*

His Society: The Psychodynamics of Primitive Social Organization, ed. Abram Kardiner (New York: Columbia University Press, 1939), p. 168.

26. Margaret Mead, *Coming of Age in Samoa* (New York: Morris Quill, 1928), p. 136.

27. Margaret Mead, *Growing Up in New Guinea* (New York: Morris Quill, 1930), p. 166.

28. Robert Suggs, "Marquesas Sexual Behavior," Yale University, unpublished paper, 1963.

29. Bronislaw Malinowski, *The Sexual Life of Savages in Northwestern Melanesia* (New York: Horace Liveright, 1929), p. 476.

30. Peter, Prince of Greece. *A Study of Polyandry* (The Hague: Monton & Co., 1963), p. 377.

31. John Honigman, *Culture and Ethos of Kaska Society* (New Haven: Yale University Press, 1949).

32. Willilam Murray, "Rowanduz: A Kurdish Administrative and Mercantile Center" (Ph.D. diss., University of Michigan, 1953), p. 263.

33. Norma Diamond, *Kún Shen: A Taiwan Village* (New York: Holt, Rinehart, & Winston, 1969), p. 34.

34. Gerardo Reichel-Dolmatoff, *The Kogi: A Tribe of the Sierra Nevada de Santa Marta* (Bogota: El Instituto Ethnologico Nacional, 1951), p. 284.

35. Dube, *Indian Village,* p. 193.

36. Jomo Kenyatta, *Facing Mount Kenya* (London: Secker & Warburg, 1953), p. 162.

37. John Morris, *Living with Lepchas: A Book About the Sikkim Himalayas* (London: Wm. Heinemann Ltd., 1938), p. 237.

38. Verrier Elwin, *The Muria and Their Gotul* (Bombay: Oxford University Press, 1947), p. 446.

39. Firth, *We the Tikopia.*

40. Colin Turnbull, *Wayward Servants: The Two Worlds of the African Pygmies* (Garden City, N.Y.: Natural History Press, 1965), p. 21.

41. Geza Roheim, *The Eternal Ones of the Dream* (New York: International Universities Press, 1945), p. 160.

42. E. E. Evans-Pritchard, *Witchcraft among the A-Zande* (Oxford: Clarendon Press, 1937), p. 174.

43. Thomas Gladwin and Seymour Sarason, *Truk: Man in Paradise* (New York: Wennen-Gren Foundation for Anthropological Research # 20, 1953), p. 115.

44. Firth, *We the Tikopia*, p. 495.

45. Heli Alzate, "Sexual Behavior of Unmarried Colombian University Students: A Follow-Up," *Archives of Sexual Behavior* 18 (1989): 239–50.

46. David Chan, "Sex Knowledge, Attitudes, and Experiences of Chinese Medical Students in Hong Kong," *Archives of Sexual Behavior* 19 (1990): 73–94.

47. K. Nagoa, poster presentation at the Twelfth World Congress on Sexology, Yokohama, Japan, August 1995.

48. S. Pongthai, poster presentation at the Twelfth World Congress on Sexology, Yokohama, Japan, August, 1995.

49. Robert Francoeur, ed., *International Encyclopedia of Sexuality* (New York: Continuum, 1997).

50. James Edwards, "The Exotic Other: Koro and the Retractile Penis," paper presented at the Twelfth World Congress on Sexology, Yokohama, Japan, August, 1995.

51. Philip Belcastro, "Sexual Behavior Differences Between Black and White Students," *Journal of Sex Research* 21 (1985): 56–67.

52. Martin Weinberg and Colin Williams, "Black Sexuality: A Test of Two Theories," *Journal of Sex Research* 25 (1988): 197–218.

53. Edward Laumann, John Gagnon, Robert Michael, et al., *The Social Organization of Sexuality* (Chicago: University of Chicago Press, 1994), p. 82.

54. See John Gagnon, "The Explicit and Implicit Use of the Scripting Perspective in Sex Research," *Annual Review of Sex Research* 1 (1990): 1–43.

55. See William Simon, "Deviance As History: The Failure of Perversion," *Archives of Sexual Behavior* 23 (1994): 1–21.

56. James Hillman, "Toward an Archetypal Model for the Masturbation Inhibition," in *Loose Ends* (Dallas: Spring Publications, 1975), pp. 105–25.

Chapter Six

■

Sin

■

In the Beginning was the Word, and the Word was that Sex was a Necessary Evil.

Religion is a powerful factor in the evolution of attitudes about sexual practices in any culture, and it has certainly been so in Western society. Our tradition of sex negativity predates Judeo-Christian thinking by thousands of years. Examples of this include the Platonic notion that sexuality is inferior to spirituality and the open hostility to bodily pleasure espoused by Greek Stoics and other ascetics.[1] The keystone in this tradition is the "split" of spiritual and physical, soul and body, God and man, good and evil, divine and mortal, sacred and profane, creative and destructive, life and death. This split is black and white, opposite and extreme, and the poles are mutually exclusive. I am not enough of a philosopher or semanticist to argue the subtle differences among dualism, duality, and dichotomy, so I have elected to avoid all these terms and speak only of the mind-body split. This split was clear in the writings of the ancient Greeks and undoubtedly existed even earlier that than that. The world was divided into spiritual and physical forces, the one good and the other evil. The soul was punished by being tied to the flesh, and the road to salvation was to escape this bondage and to become godlike. Gods were immortal and did not need to eat or to reproduce, so the path to godliness was through renunciation of the pleasures of the flesh and mortification of the body. To fast and to abstain was the road to salvation. Even though they rejected sexual pleasure, the ancients did acknowledge that the reproductive process was necessary in order to provide future generations of mortals who might then continue the quest for spiritual immortality.

Monotheistic Judeo-Christian thinking is firmly rooted in this philosophical split. The "Original Sin" was to have been born human, that is, as a result of sexual intercourse, and to have physical needs, wants, and desires. To be "saved" from this "fall from grace" required renunciation of these physical constraints in pursuit of divine spirituality. In the acknowledgement of the need for reproductive sexuality, another split developed: natural versus unnatural sexual behavior. Natural sexual behavior was based on the command to "be fruitful and multiply."[2] In this view, the natural purpose of sex is reproduction, and nonreproductive sex is therefore unnatural. This was reinforced by the mistaken observation that lower animals in their "natural" state had sex only for procreation.

The citing of biblical passages in support of a particular philosophical position about sexuality is an indoor sport rivaling sex itself in its variety and intensity. For example, a reading of the biblical text does not reveal what the people of Gomorrah did to incite the wrath of God, but the Sodomites asked Lot to bring forth his male companions "that we may know them."[3] Fire and brimstone were the punishment for this "sodomy." Whatever "sodomy" was became the basis for later condemnation of homosexuality. After Lot's wife turned into a pillar of salt for looking back on Sodom, his daughters got him drunk in order that "we may preserve the seed of our father" and he should get them pregnant. Fire and brimstone did not follow this incest. Apparently anything in the service of pregnancy and the propagation of the race was acceptable.

The Bible is silent about masturbation. Was it an unthinkable activity, unimportant, or acceptable under the law? The much maligned "sin of Onan" occurred when Onan "spilled his seed on the ground" rather than impregnate Tamar, widow of his dead brother.[4] The latter was a religious requirement of the time. "Coitus interruptus" as a method of birth control apparently angered God, who slew Onan. This was a heavy price to pay for pulling out early. The message was that sex was for procreation, not pleasure, even if Onan wasn't having any fun. Semen had to be used for the natural act of making babies. It has been suggested that the proper interpretation of this passage is that an authoritarian God punished Onan for violating religious law and that he made no judgment about sexual practice per se, be it masturbation or birth control. We note that later, Tamar dressed up as a prostitute and got Onan's father Judah to impregnate her.[5] Neither of them was slain and the propagation of the race went on. Among nomadic tribes, including the ancient Jews, the most numerous tribe was the strongest and there was therefore a premium on procreation. Such unlimited fertility was also correlated with high child mortality and expansionism. This biblical standard reflects the time in which it was written and is not necessarily relevant today.

The Christian contribution to the Bible was no more specific about sexual practices than was the Judaic. It also contained the same splits. Jesus said, "Render therefore unto Caesar the things which are Caesar's and unto God the things that are God's."[6] Paul was a prolific letter writer and it was he who was usually cited and interpreted in the subsequent unfolding of "natural law" regarding sexuality. In Rom. 1:27, Paul referred to "the natural use of women," and in Gal. 5:19, "Now the works of the flesh are manifest, which are these: Adultery, fornication, uncleanliness, lasciviousness." In Gal. 6:8 he noted that, "For he that soweth to his flesh shall of the flesh reap corruption; but he that soweth to the Spirit shall of the Spirit reap life-everlasting." The flesh was corrupt, but some "natural" activity had to take place if the race were to go on. Christianity taught that one attained spirituality by accepting the word of the scripture as delivered by church authority. Adherence to the rules, mortification of the flesh, and renunciation of physical pleasures were the road to salvation.

In his very influential writings, Augustine referred to Paul as "The Apostle" and cited him frequently. About 400 C.E., when he was Bishop of Hippo, Augustine wrote his *Confessions*. Here was a man who knew guilt, talking to his God. Augustine was clear in his evolution: "But I wretched, most wretched, in the very commencement of my early youth, had begged chastity of Thee and said, 'Give me chastity and continency, only not yet.' For I feared lest Thou shouldest hear me soon, and cure me of the disease of concupiscence which I wished to have satisfied rather than extinguished."[7] Later, his concupiscence, defined as strong desire or lust, was controlled in all matters of the flesh, including eating, drinking, and especially "lust of the eyes" or the pleasure in looking at the world. Augustine never accepted responsibility for his own sexuality and, instead, blamed his anxiety about it on the evil pleasure of sex itself. It was Augustine, apparently, who coined the term "Original Sin" and put fig leaves on Adam and Eve. He himself had been schooled in the tradition of Manichaean dualism and easily embraced the concept that sex is evil. By attributing it to Paul, he managed to avoid responsibility again.

In *The City of God*, Augustine suggested that it would be

ideal if "the man then, would have sown the seed and the woman received it, as need required, the generative organs being moved by the will, not excited by lust." Augustine likened that process to farting: "Some have such command of their bowels, that they can break wind continuously at plea-sure, so as to produce the effect of singing."[8] He apparently could not appreciate that playing the Gloria on the anal organ would be any fun. As much as he said about lust, Augustine never specifically said anything about masturbation.

Masturbation as sin came to be based on the sixth com-mandment, "Thou shalt not commit adultery." Originally, "adultery" referred only to intercourse with someone else's wife and it was a crime against property. If the other woman was not married, the sin was "fornication." When married couples got beyond child-bearing age, marital sex itself became sinful as well. Semen was "seed" and, as such, had to be sown for only one purpose, procreation. Depositing it in the wrong vessel or outside the vessel was a mortal sin. Over time, "adultery" thus expanded to include fornication, postmenopausal sex, coitus interruptus, masturbation, oral and anal sex, and bestiality. The early church fathers believed that the semen, like the proverbial mustard seed, contained the entire germ of life and was essentially a little person planted in the fertile field of the uterus. In this they chose to follow the Aristotelian rather than the Diocle-sian/Hippocratic view, which postulated that both parents contributed seed. The discovery of spermatozoa in 1677 and the ovum in 1827 ended this preformation versus epigenesis debate and changed reproductive physiology but had no effect on religious dogma.

As the early church evolved, personal mortification in reparation for sin with sackcloth, ashes, fasting, and prayer gave way to confession and absolution by a priest. This cre-ated an obvious demand for a penalty list. Beginning in the fifth century, there were penitential books to guide confessors in their task. Potential penance included reading psalms, fasting, vigils, whipping, pilgrimages, and restitution. To put masturbation in perspective as a relatively minor league vice, consider some early examples. Cummean, in Irish penitentials circa 650, recommended fasting and asking pardon of God on an hourly basis as the standard penance. For "natural fornication" (i.e., with a woman), this penance would last for seven years; for "sodomy," seven years; for "befouling the lips," four years; but for "sin with the self," three forty-day periods. Theodore, the Archbishop of Canterbury circa 690, gave penance of one year for fornication with a virgin, three years with a married woman, ten to fifteen years with a man or beast, but only forty days for "defiling himself." Boys who mutually engaged in the vice were to be whipped but apparently not required to do other penance.[9]

While the monks in the British Isles were providing penitents with a way to be absolved of sexual defilement and to participate again in the sacraments, the churchmen on the Continent were making lists of rules or canons to govern the church as a whole and to regulate the behaviors of its members. These were gathered into the so-called Gratian Decrees in 1140. The early canonists had little interest in sexual matters beyond the determination that only married couples could have sex and then only to conceive children. Marriage occurred once in a lifetime. Even when revised in 1917, Canon Law held firmly to the principle that "the primary end of marriage is the procreation and education of children."[10] From this simple rule, all the prohibitions on nonprocreative sexual activity flow naturally.

Confessors were supposed to ask about sexual activities, and their obsessive pursuit of the details of sexual sins was a clear manifestation of the principle widely attributed to Pope Gregory I that sexual pleasure could never be without sin.[11] If orgasm were pleasurable, then it was sinful. Sexual pleasure was a motherlode of confessional gold.

   Thirteenth-century theologian Albertus Magnus and his pupil Thomas Aquinas believed that sexual pleasure might actually serve the goal of propagation, but they still believed that it was sinful. Aquinas's *Summa Theologica,* circa 1270, extended the sex negativity propounded by Augustine. Aquinas carried the concept of what was natural or unnatural about sex to new heights of logical rationality—or irrationality, as the case might be. Natural sex had to be procreative. Thus Aquinas argued that fornication was more natural and less sinful than sodomy or bestiality. It was even less sinful to have intercourse with one's mother than to masturbate; apparently, only if mother were past childbearing age would such incest be unnatural. Aquinas also believed that intercourse in other than the male-superior position (later encouraged by missionaries and known thereafter as the "missionary position") was sinful. The seed might otherwise spill out and "wrong" positions were therefore seen as forms of contraception.[12] Aquinas's views of women as inferior and as servant of man may have a role here as well. He could not accept women on top under any circumstances.

   Aquinas's most tragic contribution to Catholic doctrine was the demonization of sex. He believed that the devil had power over the sexual function of men and was therefore responsible for impotence. The devil worked through witches/women. If witches caused men to be impotent, then that was a form of contraception and was therefore unnatural and sinful. In 1484, Pope Innocent VIII cited Aquinas and, in the "Witches' Bull," declared that "the power of the Devil lies in the privy parts of men."[13] Under papal authority then, the Inquisition rooted out all the handmaidens of the devil, those witches who tempted or failed to satisfy men and were therefore responsible for their sexual behaviors and misadventures. Torture produced confession of sins. The penalty for such sins was death.

In 1215, the Fourth Lateran Council had created the obligation to confess sins at least once a year. Over time, the focus shifted from the sexual acts themselves to the circumstances of sex. An "examination of conscience" before confession thus shifted the locus of control from an external to an internal regulation of sexuality. As precursors of sexual activity, desire and fantasy were evil in themselves and led to a loss of control and to hyperexcitability. Thus the preceding physical setting or psychic mindset became the "occasion of sin" and as bad as the act of sin itself.

Catholicism does not seem to have evolved much in the last four hundred years. "Masturbation" is not even listed in *Sacramentum Mundi*, a Catholic encyclopedia. Alphabetically, nothing comes between "mass stipend" and "materialism," an observation that probably speaks for itself. The word does appear under "sex." "Masturbation as a form of sexual satisfaction outside marriage, widely practiced by young people, should be regarded to a great extent as a transitional phase of sexual development or a reaction to the tension of a strained atmosphere . . . it cannot be regarded as a fully proper form of sexual activity."[14] In *A Catholic Parent's Guide to Sex Education* (1962) the author cautions that "Masturbation, or self-abuse . . . is a voluntary action and is, quite obviously, a grave sin. . . . It should be explained that the ability to perform the sexual act has been given solely for the purpose of having intercourse with a woman so that she may conceive a child and that any other use of it is an abuse of one of God's greatest gifts."[15] In *Sex Education in the Family*, Father Francis Filas notes that "masturbation is considered in itself something morally wrong: this would be a misuse of the sexual powers, which are to be used solely between husband and wife in their marriage."[16] Finally, Reginald Trevett wrote that "we have to help the young to achieve true, vital chastity in spite of masturbation."[17]

As far as we know, no pope since the early Middle Ages

has engaged in "sperm wars" but the act-centered construct of human sexuality remains unchanged. The word from late-twentieth-century popes, the last absolute monarchs in the Western world, has been sparse but consistent. Pius XII in a radio address in 1952 said that the demand for divine purity of body and mind retained its full force and that it was possible for adolescents to attain purity. Paul VI, in *Humanae Vitae* in 1968, wrote that man has no domination over his generative faculties as such because of their intrinsic ordination toward raising up life, of which God is the principle. Paul VI also wrote in *Declaration on Some Questions of Sexual Ethics* in 1975 that masturbation was a grave sin "even though it is not possible to prove unequivocally that Holy Scripture expressly repudiates this sin as such." The post-Vatican II 1983 revision of Canon Law to provide for "the good of the spouses" before "the procreation and education of offspring" in the matrimonial covenant did nothing to reverse other sexual prohibitions. The 1994 *New Catechism* states that among the sins gravely contrary to chastity were masturbation, fornication, pornography, and homosexual practice. John Paul II in *The Splendor of Truth* in 1993 wrote that homosexuality, masturbation, premarital sex, abortion, and sterilization lie outside the natural order created by God and such "sexual sins" are "morally unacceptable."[18]

Like the ancient tribes, today's church believes that there is strength in numbers and that procreation is therefore the only rightful purpose for sexual behavior.

While the concept of sin remains alive and well, there is still hope. Catholics can still go to confession, do penance, and be absolved. Their milk-bottle souls can be all white again, for those of us who recall that image from the First Catechism. Thankfully, there are still guidebooks to help the confessor determine how many laps around the rosary are appropriate for each maleficent act. *Counselling the Catholic*, a 1959 manual by priests for priests, first disposed of the argument that masturbation was normal. "Considering the near universality of the phenomenon, it is easy to see why some psychologists have confused frequency with normality." Although they occur very infrequently, there are individuals who appear to develop to maturity without having masturbated. Statistics and probability theory aside, then "the moral theologian is quite right in insisting that masturbation is not, per se, an inherent and necessary characteristic of normal development. . . . Theologians are in unanimous agreement that masturbation is always objectively a grave sin, for whatever purpose it is committed." However, "sexual passion, when thoroughly aroused, can overpower human freedom," and "inveterate habits of impurity lead us to suspect that grave subjective guilt may possibly be absent."[19] These are definitions of overpowering passion and compulsive masturbation. Lawyers will recognize these as the "irresistible impulse" and "not guilty by reason of insanity" defenses. Imagine a lawyer in the confessional: "Father, if my client admits that he masturbated three times on Thursday, but he couldn't help himself, can we plea bargain for five Our Fathers and three Hail Marys?" The suggested approach to counseling the sinner is to focus on the "healthy Catholic attitude toward sex," that is, "the true, outgoing, giving and sharing love of marriage."

By now some of us have been wondering about those priests, the middlemen who dole out the penance and follow the word sent down from on high. Theirs is a higher calling as Trevett said. "A study of the realities involved in marriage helps us to understand why the Church holds consecrated virginity to be the higher state."[20] The married "subdue the urges of passion" in their work as parents while the virginal are wholly occupied in the worship and contemplation of God. So, just what do those consecrated, virginal celibate priests who tell us what we should do, actually do themselves?

In 1990, Richard Sipe, a "retired" priest, published his work, *A Secret World*, in determining how "celibacy" was conceptualized and practiced. He gathered information about the sex lives of fifteen hundred priests over a twenty-five year period. Some priests were in therapy, some spoke up at workshops or retreats, and some information was shared by participants in or observers of priestly sexuality. This was not a scientific survey where "cultural scorn" would be writ large. Such surveys have been done and no priest acknowledged a problem with either alcohol or sex. Because of their personal relationship with the surveyor, participants in the Sipe study probably were truthful, and that data are probably the most accurate that we have to date. The ideal celibate renounces the flesh in his quest for spirituality. Masturbation may be labeled as pathological, immature, and sinful, but 80 percent of the clergy surveyed masturbated at least occasionally.[21]

Sipe found several subgroups of priests who masturbated. Some simply liked priestly work, and celibacy was not a spiritual ideal. These men used masturbation to relieve sexual tension and to avoid other sexual entanglements. Some denied their sexuality or argued that what they did—such as no hands—was not really masturbation. Some were hypocrites, masturbating to fantasy, yet condemning the practice in others. Some rationalized that if they resisted the temptation a certain number of times, then it was not sinful to give in to the urge the next time. Some saw masturbation as the lesser of two evils and as a substitute for sexual activity with another person. Some were gentle and reasonable with flaws in themselves, as they were with the flaws in others. Finally, there were some who saw masturbation as a virtue.

In the view of the last group, a priest could identify himself with Christ as a human being by giving himself up to God in acknowledgement of his own humanity. As a man, Jesus had a 95 percent probability of having masturbated. "Masturbation can be an expression of maturity at any age and, at times may be virtuous." Sex is viewed as part of the nature of man and is not tinged with evil. While individual priests may hold such a gentle, "Christ-like" view of masturbation, this is obviously not the official position of the Catholic Church. As in so many other ways, here the institutional church differs from the people of the church.

Another male-dominated, authoritarian, hierarchical group, the Mormons, has equally strong views. Spencer Kimball wrote in *The Miracle of Forgiveness,* in a chapter called "Crimes against Nature," (there's a clue), that "prophets anciently and today condemn masturbation. It induces feelings of guilt and shame. It is detrimental to spirituality. It indicates slavery to the flesh, not that mastery of it and the growth toward godhood which is the object of our mortal life. . . . While we should not regard this weakness as the heinous sin which some other sexual practices are, it is of itself bad enough to require sincere repentance. What is more, it too often leads to grievous sin, even to that sin against nature homosexuality."[22] As archaic an idea as this is, it was written in 1969; however, the program to stamp out masturbation must have been successful because the latest Mormon missionary at the door told me that there are no homosexuals in the Church of Jesus Christ of Latter Day Saints. Apparently, he had been told not to discuss this, and the national gay and lesbian Mormon group, Affirmation, would disagree with him anyway.

Religious groups with less hierarchy and structure seem less condemnatory. A 1991 statement on human sexuality by the General Assembly of the Presbyterian Church (U.S.A.) said that children and young people should explore the pleasure of their bodies without shame or guilt: "Masturbation enables teens to experience sexual pleasure and become familiar with their own sexual response." There was not a general acceptance of adult masturbation; however, the physically disabled "should have permission and encouragement to experiment with pleasurable and nonex-ploitive sexual experiences," the mentally retarded should be allowed to have "self-pleasuring [when] appropriate and possible," and the elderly without partners should be able to satisfy their sexual needs.[23]

Other Protestant denominations continue to struggle with position statements on sexuality. The Lutherans were debating the normality of masturbation as this was being written. Other groups have avoided commitment.

At the opposite end of the spectrum, a Unitarian Univer-salist pamphlet, *About Your Sexuality*, written by Derek Calderwood in 1983, observed that masturbation "is a life-long form of sexual expression enjoyable at any age and is appropriate whether one has a regular partner or not."[24]

There is a relationship between authoritarian control and the prohibition of individual freedom and pleasure, regardless of the inability of some preachers to practice their own rules. This is consistent with survey data by both Kinsey and Hunt which showed that negative feelings about sexuality were correlated with church attendance, espe-cially if that church was fundamentalist in its perspective. The notions that masturbation is unnatural, sinful, or symp-tomatic of personal crisis are pervasive in religiously ori-ented thought. Guilt is an institutionalized social construct. The concept that masturbation may be virtue itself has far from general acceptance, but if enough of us truly believe in our virtue, then there is potential for institutional change.

In one early Egyptian creation myth, the god Khepera, having produced himself from primal matter, then mastur-bated the world into existence. "He hath thrust his member into his hand, and hath performed his desire, and hath pro-duced the children Shu and Tefnut."[25] Like Adam and Eve, they went on to reproduce in the usual way. On the other side of the world, the Kuna of Panama also had a creation story that people were created by masturbation of the Sun god.[26] Imagine how different the world of sexuality might have been if this myth had caught on rather than the one about mud and ribs.

NOTES

1. Vern Bullough and Bonnie Bullough, *Sin, Sickness, and Sanity* (New York: Garland, 1977).

2. Gen. 9:1.

3. Gen. 19:5.

4. Gen. 38:9.

5. Gen. 38:18.

6. Matt. 22:21.

7. Augustine of Hippo, *Confessions* VIII:17.

8. Augustine of Hippo, *City of God* XIV:24.

9. John McNeill and Helen Ganner, *Medieval Handbooks of Penance* (New York: Octagon, 1965).

10. Canon 1013.

11. Uta Ranke-Heinemann, *Eunuchs for the Kingdom of Heaven: Women, Sexuality, and the Catholic Church* (New York: Penguin, 1990), p. 137.

12. Thomas Aquinas, *Summa Theologica* (New York: Benziger Bros., 1914).

13. Ranke-Heinemann, *Eunuchs for the Kingdom of Heaven*, p. 153.

14. Karl Rahner, ed., *Sacramentum Mundi* (New York: Herder & Herder, 1970), p. 85

15. Audrey Kelly, *A Catholic Parent's Guide to Sex Education* (New York: Hawthorn, 1962), p. 59.

16. Francis Filas, *Sex Education in the Family* (Englewood Cliffs, N.J.: Prentice-Hall, 1966), p. 87.

17. Reginald Trevett, *The Church and Sex* (New York: Hawthorn, 1960), p. 91.

18. See Thomas Fox, *Sexuality and Catholicism* (New York: George Braziller, 1995) for extensive comments on papal thinking.

19. George Hagmaier and Robert Gleason, *Counselling the Catholic* (New York: Sheed and Ward, 1959).

20. Trevett, *The Church and Sex*, p. 41.

21. A. W. Richard Sipe, *A Secret World: Sexuality and the Search for Celibacy* (New York: Brunner/Mazel, 1990).

22. Spencer Kimball, *The Miracle of Forgiveness* (Salt Lake City: Bookcraft, 1969), p. 77.

23. Office of the General Assembly of the Presbyterian Church (U.S.A.), *Decisions of the 203rd General Assembly on Sexuality* (Louisville, Ky., 1991), chap. 3.

24. Derek Calderwood, *About Your Sexuality* (Boston: Unitarian Universalist Association, 1983).

25. E. A. Wallis Budge, *The Gods of the Egyptians*, vol. 1 (London: Methuen & Co., 1904), p. 297.

26. Regina Hollomon, *Developmental Changes in San Blas* (Ann Arbor, Mich.: University Microfilm International, 1969), p. 231.

Chapter Seven

■

Sickness

■

Historically, the view that masturbation would cause eternal damnation in the next life was supported by the view that it caused disease in this one. The medical view of masturbation has evolved along with medicine itself. In ancient times, "patients" visited temples of healing where they slept in order to be cured by gods, and then they left an offering of thanks at the door. Today, patients visit modern, high-tech, scientific temples of healing where they leave their insurance information at the door before they are admitted in order to be cured by "gods" in white coats or green scrub suits. Patients have progressed from being carried in on a shield to being admitted on an insurance card in only three thousand years.

Medically speaking, masturbation was considered normal and not a problem for millennia until it was "discovered" about three hundred years ago that it was the cause of most of the physical and mental illnesses then known to man. If illness had not been caused by the devil, then it had surely been caused by masturbation. "Masturbation insanity" had become a major concern by the early

111

nineteenth century. After the acceptance of the germ theory later in that century, "masturbation neurosis" or neurasthenia was the residual concern. Advances in psychology and in the isolation of hormones in the early twentieth century redefined masturbation not as the cause, but rather as a symptom of underlying emotional problems. With further observation and reflection, the view has come full circle to the acceptance of masturbation as normal behavior.

In primitive societies, wounds and broken bones heal mechanically with the aid of thread or splints, simple problems respond to herbs and potions, and complex problems of unknown cause require magical or supernatural cures. Western society follows that tradition. In temples dedicated to the Greek god/man Aesclepius (identified by snake and staff), the complexly afflicted came to sleep and to be visited in their dreams by curing gods. In the fifth century B.C.E., the physician Hippocrates believed in natural cause and cure, made clinical observations, and wrote about those observations. Medicine was the "science" of humors, spirits, and vapors. The humors were liquids that flowed from the body and were assumed to be in balance within it; the spirits or vital essences were other fluids in the body that aided in that balance; vapors were external fluids, such as dampness in the night air, which put the system out of balance.

Galen, a Roman physician of the second century, C.E., codified the humors as blood, phlegm, yellow bile, and black bile. He noted seasonal variations and constitutional types as well. His texts were influential for the next fifteen hundred years. There were two major reasons for this. First, scholars tended to refer exclusively to authority and not to make fresh and independent observations. Second, the church forbade dissection and discouraged scientific study. Galen's medical interventions balanced the humors by bleeding out bad blood, purging black bile, diuresing (urinating) yellow bile, and expectorating phlegm. This was the standard medical practice for centuries. Vital essences were extremely important and they had to be in balance and not wasted.

Around 1700, "Dr. Bekker," probably a Dutch clergyman, wrote a pamphlet with the impressive title (in part), "Onania or the Heinous Sin of Self-Pollution and All Its Frightful Consequences in both sexes, considered with Spiritual and Physical Advice to Those who have already Injured themselves by this Abominal Practice." It was Bekker who coined the term "Sin of Onan." The consequences were terrible, but the treatment mild as it included meditation, diet, exercise, and marriage.[1] The pamphlet might have passed into well-deserved, ignominious obscurity had it not been for Dr. Samuel Auguste André David Tissot. A devout Catholic, this Swiss physician wrote *Tentamen deo Morbis ex Manustrupatione*, or *A Treatise on the Diseases Produced by Onanism*, in 1758. He referred at length to the writings of Hippocrates, Galen, and Bekker in characterizing the diseases: All the intellectual faculties are enfeebled, the powers of the body fail entirely, acute pains supervene, pimples appear, the organs of generation are affected, and intestinal function is deranged. Tissot painted a picture of an Onanist as

> a general wasting of the animal machine, a debility of all the body senses, and of all the faculties of the mind, the loss of the imagination and of the memory; imbecility; the shame and disgrace attendant upon it, all the functions disturbed, suspended, or painful; long, severe and disgusting diseases, a pain sharper and constantly recurring; all the diseases of old age in the period of vigor; an inaptitude for all the occupations for which man was born; the humiliating thought of being only a useless weight upon the earth; the disgust for all honorable pleasures; weariness, an aversion for others and for himself; horror of life, and the dread of someday committing suicide, anguish of mind worse that the pains, and remorse worse than the anguish, which increases daily and doubtless assumes new power, when the soul is enfeebled only by attachment

to the body, will serve perhaps for eternal punishment, and unquenchable fire.[2]

Tissot was no less colorful in describing the problems for women:

> Besides all the symptoms we have mentioned, they are particularly subject to attacks of hysteria, melancholy, incurable jaundice, acute pains in the stomach and back, *fluor albus*, the acridity of which is a constant source of acute suffering, prolapsus and ulceration of the uterus and their consequences, to elongations of the clitoris and furor uteranus which deprives them of modesty and reason and places them on a level with the most lacivious brutes, until death terminates their career.[3]

Tissot referred to Hippocrates as his authority for the results of "too much evacuation of seminal fluid." Hippocrates had attributed this to "excess venery," which was too much intercourse and not masturbation, but this detail did not appear to bother Tissot. In the chapter "Importance of Semen," he noted that the seminal fluid was the "animal spirit" or "spinal marrow" taken by both brain and testicles from all the humors of the body that would better have been enriched by its retention. "The symptoms which supervene in females are explained like those in men. The secretion which they lose, being less valuable and less natural than the semen of the male, its loss does not enfeeble so promptly, but when they indulge in it to excess, as their nervous system is naturally weaker and more disposed to spasm, the symptoms are more violent."[4] The example he then used was that of a prostitute who had "connection with six Spanish dragoons" in a single night and bled to death of uterine hemorrhage the next morning. Tissot never explained how this could be related to masturbation. Loss of the "animal spirit" caused "dorsal consumption" or weakness, debility, immobility, convulsions, emaciation, dryness, pain in the membranes of the brain, and impaired senses, especially sight. Tissot added Bekker's insanity, blindness, consumption, clap, pox, tumors, hemorrhoids, and death to complete the picture. He ignored Galen's idea that masturbation might actually be helpful in order to get rid of bad humors. If one subscribes to the humoral theory, as Tissot did, then it made sense to try to prevent imbalances. Bleeding, diarrhea, vomiting, and excessive perspiration were obvious symptoms of dysfunctional output which the physician tried to cure by changing input of food, fluid, and potions. A patient might not be able to control his diarrhea, but he ought to be able to control his seminal excretions. Besides that, a powerful orgasm could be exhausting. Today, we tend not to see that as pathology.

Further modern digression is in order at this point. Tissot appeared to be aware of the connection between sex and some symptoms of clap (gonorrhea) and pox (syphilis) but he did not conceive of these as sexually transmitted diseases. He misinterpreted the milky discharge of gonorrhea as a chronic loss of seminal fluid, a sort of inability to turn off the faucet after it had been turned on by masturbation. Most of the symptoms that refer to the spinal cord and brain, including blindness, epilepsy, dementia, and movement disorders, are characteristic of tertiary syphilis and now known as *general paresis* and *tabes dorsalis*. The weakness and debilitating respiratory symptoms of "consumption" are now recognized as tuberculosis, which is not a sexually transmitted disease. If Tissot's patients had limited their sexual activity to masturbation, then they would not have acquired the symptoms which he ascribed to that activity.

As had Bekker, Tissot offered a treatment: chinchona, febrifuge, and cold baths. He also recommended sleep, exercise, especially walks and horseback rides in the country air (better vapor), and a diet of broth, no fruits, and milk. He speculated that milk from a woman might be the best therapy but he discouraged it because going to the nipple might excite too much passion.

It would be a mistake to underestimate the influence of Tissot, as his work was published until 1905. In the preface to the 1832 American edition, the anonymous translator, identified only as "a physician from the Medical Society of the city and county of New York," stated that his intent was "to direct the attention of the profession to the alarmingly pernicious effects of onanism, or to warn the miserable subject of it, of the truly deplorable situation into which he is plunging himself." Both the physicians and the miserable subjects got the message.

Benjamin Rush had probably read Tissot when he was a medical student in Edinburgh. The most influential physician in America in the late eighteenth century, Rush is now remembered as a signer of the Declaration of Independence, a founder of American psychiatry, and the man who bled George Washington to death while balancing his humors. In 1812 Rush wrote *Medical Inquiries and Observations upon the Diseases of the Mind*. He believed that madness was a disorder of the blood vessels of the brain and he placed the blame squarely on onanism: "The morbid effects of intemperance in a sexual intercourse with women are feeble, and of a transient nature, compared with the train of physical and moral evils which this solitary vice fixes upon the mind and body."[5] Rush's oft-quoted list of evils included

seminal weakness, impotence, dysury [painful urination], *tabes dorsalis* [syphilis], pulmonary consumption [tuberculosis], dyspepsia [stomach disorders], dimness of sight, vertigo, epilepsy, hypochondriasis, loss of memory, manalgia [depression], fatuity [dementia], and death. . . . But these are not all the melancholy and disgusting effects of excess in the indulgence of the sexual appetite. They sometimes discover themselves in the imagination and senses, in a fondness for obscene conversation and books, and in a wanton dalliance with women, long after the ability to gratify the appetite has perished from disease or age.[6]

To cure this state of physical, mental, and moral degeneracy, Rush recommended a vegetable diet, temperance, bodily labor, cold baths, avoidance of obscenity, music, a close study of mathematics, military glory, and, if all else failed, castor oil.

So far in our history, the consequences of masturbation have been horrible but the treatment humane and mild. The advanced physical ills could not be cured but the patient was treated with compassion. This focus changed in the latter half of the last century with two related breakthroughs in medicine, the acceptance of the germ theory and the development of social hygiene (later known as preventive medicine).

Louis Pasteur proved that microorganisms or bacteria were responsible for fermentation and for infectious disease, and he successfully experimented with vaccination against sheep anthrax in 1881 and rabies in 1885. Robert Koch cultured and stained bacteria to make them visible under a microscope, tuberculosis in 1882 and cholera in 1883. With the eventual discovery of *Treponema pallidum* (syphilis) and *Neisseria gonorrhoeae* (gonorrhea), it was no longer possible to blame those physical ills caused by germs on the evils of masturbation. The belief that semen was the vital fluid of masculinity persisted in some writings until the isolation of the hormone testosterone in 1935.

Once physical degeneracy had been attributed to germs and vital essences had been expunged from the medical texts, the only conditions still attributable to the evils of masturbation were mental and moral degeneracy.

If germs were responsible for disease, then it became possible to prevent contact with those germs and to prevent the disease. Joseph Lister introduced barriers during surgery and Pasteur introduced the process of boiling or pasteurization. Unfortunately, the social hygiene concept of disease prevention was expanded to include the suppression of masturbation in order to prevent mental and moral breakdown.

Some of the preventionists followed the example of Rush and focused on diet, exercise, and sexual abstinence. One of these was evangelist, prohibitionist, and vegetarian Sylvester Graham. Graham believed that eating meat increased one's carnal desire so he proposed a diet of vegetables and whole grain bread in order to decrease passion. Eating Graham's crackers was supposed to promote sexual abstinence. Graham was followed by John Harvey Kellogg, M.D., who also promoted nutrition, exercise, and sexual abstinence at his sanitarium in Battle Creek, Michigan. Part of his program was a breakfast cereal he called Sanitas Corn Flakes. John Harvey's brother Will Keith expanded this into a whole line of breakfast cereals that bore the Kellogg family name. Dietary prevention had become part of the long-term prevention of degeneracy.[7]

Not content with the usual laundry list of dire consequences, Kellogg pointed out the "thirty-nine signs of the secret vice of self abuse" for which all right-thinking parents should be vigilant. These were general debility, early symptoms of consumption, premature puberty, sudden changes in disposition, lassitude, a dull look in the eyes, sleeplessness, forgetfulness, fickleness, untrustworthiness, love of solitude, bashfulness, unnatural boldness, mock piety, easy fright, confusion, wantonness in girls, round shoulders, weak backs, paralysis of the lower extremities, shuffling gait, bad positions in bed, lack of breast development in girls after puberty, capricious appetite, a fondness for unnatural foods (especially spices), eating clay, disgust for simple food (like corn flakes), the use of tobacco, unnatural paleness, acne, biting the fingernails, sunken eyes, heart palpitations, hysteria, menstrual irregularities, epileptic fits, wetting the bed, and unchastity of speech.[8] Kellogg obviously didn't know any normal adolescents. In fact, he had no children because, as he was proud to point out, he never had a sexual relationship with his wife.

Most of the good doctors of the late nineteenth century thought that nighttime was the period of highest risk for masturbation as well as for that other pollution, the nocturnal emission or "spermatorrhea" in the disease model. Several measures were recommended in order to prevent sexual arousal. They began with exercising in order to induce fatigue, eating bland foods for the evening meal, emptying the bladder before retiring, wearing loose clothing, sleeping on the side, and keeping the hands outside the blankets. One doctor suggested lining up all the beds in school dormitories with a wall separating the upper third from the lower two-thirds. The upper third would be kept dark to promote sleep while the lower part would be lighted and watched in order to prevent self abuse. Most trousers were made without pockets in order to prevent surreptitious fingering of the genitals. These methods were applicable to girls as well as to boys.

If such a program were unsuccessful in preventing masturbation, then more drastic methods might be necessary. In 1900 a surgeon named F. R. Sturgis suggested the following sequence: medical treatment of irritants, mechanical restraints, and surgical intervention.[9] First, mechanical problems such as bladder stones, urethral strictures, worms, rectal irritations, or an inflamed or dirty foreskin were identified and treated. Circumcision was recommended for the latter and it was done without anesthesia in order that pain be a lesson to the self-abuser.

Absent physical evidence of irritation, the physician proceeded to strategies that would prevent the fingering of the genitals in order to produce orgasm. Mechanical restraints were used primarily at night but could also be applied during the day in particularly difficult cases.

Devices included straitjackets to restrict the arms and hands, bandages on the penis, leather gloves locked together at the wrists, a close-meshed wire cage from waist to thighs, and other forms of anti-masturbatory armor. These chastity belt–like devices were often locked in order to prevent tampering by the wearer. For girls, "chastity belts" prevented both intercourse and masturbation. For boys, double-sided splints might be applied to the penis or a ring with nails protruding through to the inside put over it. If the penis swelled in erection, then the nails would press into the flesh and awaken and alert the wearer to the danger as well as cause detumescence. A sling might hold the penis down and back between the legs so that erection was painful. Cooling devices using water or metal were supposed to decrease arousal.

At least twenty-one devices to prevent male masturbation and/or nocturnal emissions were patented in the United States between 1856 and 1932.[10] Some included electric charges or noisemakers to alert the wearer and others to the presence of an erection and to discourage self-stimulation. More extreme measures included blistering the thighs, spine, and/or genitals; injection of silver nitrate into the urethra for cauterization; and infibulation. The latter referred to several methods of fastening the foreskin together in order to prevent erection. Thread, wire, and two nickel-plated safety pins were suggested. If these measures were unsuccessful, then severing the [nonexistent] dorsal nerve of the penis, or even castration were used. From 1890 to 1925, there was a medical group in the United States, the Orificial Surgical Society, which specialized in such operations.[11] They seemed especially keen to operate on girls, removing the clitoris, excising labia, and even cauterizing the vagina. Mutilation of genital openings in the pursuit of the prevention of masturbation was condoned in the misguided hope of preventing insanity. This must remain one of the low points in the history of American medicine.

The Victorian-Edwardian view of sexuality was a strangely sentimentalized one. Women were pure except for fallen women, children were innocent except those that had inferior constitutions, and men were responsible for preservation of the natural order of things. Masturbation led to degeneracy, both mental and moral, and there was no room for discussion. In his 1880 edition of *Pathology of Mind*, the noted English psychiatrist Henry Maudsley described "the insanity of self-abuse":

> The patient is completely wrapped up in self, egotistically insensitive to the claims of others upon him and of his duties to them, hypochondriacally occupied with his sensations and his bodily functions, abandoned to indolent and solitary self-brooding; he displays a vanity and self-sufficiency quite unbecoming his age and position; exacts the constant indulgence of others without the least thought of obligation or gratitude, and is apt, if he gets not the consideration which he claims, to declare that his family are unfeeling and do not understand him.[12]

Does this sound like the insanity of self-abuse or normal adolescence? Maudsley noted in passing that there were exceptions to the rule. "In another sort of temperament, the vice is the exciting cause of an attack of ordinary acute mania or melancholia, and it is sometimes practiced for a long time without any mental ill effects." Also "It is not certain that the vice in woman produces a form of mental disorder so characteristically featured as in men, in that it is so injurious to them."[13]

In 1880 an American, Dr. George Beard, gave the syndrome a name: neurasthenia. Anxiety, depression, fatigue, and the hypochondriasis of multiple and/or vague physical complaints were its characteristics. The hypochondria of masturbation caused many a young man to confess his vice to the "experts" and to undertake a cure. The 1884 *Boston*

Medical and Surgical Journal reported the case of a young man

> about the age of 13 years [who] began to masturbate, and, urged by his companions, he practiced at some time before he produced an emission. After that he continuted the habit more and more frequently, until he would perform the operation every day for several weeks in succession, and very often twice a day. At the age of 16 his health was so much impaired that he was obliged to suspend all labor and extended exercise. . . . I found him pale, trembling and dejected—pulse frequent and feeble, appetite bad, digestion impaired and rather emaciated.[14]

After a few bottles of "strengthening tincture," he improved. With such testimonials to patent medicines and surgery, the cure of masturbation became a big business.

In 1886 neuropsychiatrist Richard von Krafft-Ebing published his famous *Psychopathia Sexualis*. While he devoted much more space to twenty-five different fetishes, he still had harsh words for "the practice of masturbation in early years. It despoils the unfolding bud of perfume and beauty, and leaves behind only the coarse animal desire for sexual satisfaction." While the "untainted" individual might escape the awful consequences, "with tainted individuals the matter is quite different. The latent perverse sexuality is developed under the influence of neurasthenia induced by masturbation."[15]

The English physician and sexologist Havelock Ellis coined the term "autoeroticism" in his *Studies in the Psychology of Sex* in 1900. He defined it as "spontaneous sexual emotion without external stimuli" and he saw masturbation as the end point on a continuum that included nocturnal emissions and daydreaming, or "psychic onanism." Like many of his contemporaries, Ellis hedged his predictions about safety. "There appears to be little reliable evidence to show that simple masturbation, in a well-born and healthy individual, can produce any evil results beyond slight functional disturbances, and these only when it is practiced to excess."[16] "Excess" was not clearly defined except as "several times daily for several years." The examples given were ten to twenty-five times per day for five to seven years. Most of us would probably agree that this is "excess" and that there is a lot of room in the normal range. "Excess" could cause problems including "neurasthenia with its manifold symptoms, . . . inaptitude for coitus,. . . sexual inversion [homosexuality], . . . [and a] morbid heightening of self-consciousness without any coordinated heightening of self-esteem."[17] The last one sounds like guilt: "In women, I attach considerable importance, as a result of masturbation, to an aversion for normal coitus in later life."[18] Ellis did acknowledge that masturbation relieved physical oppression, sexual tension, and mental obsessions which were the inevitable result of the perpetual restraints of our civilized life.[19]

Both Ellis and Krafft-Ebing recognized that not all youthful masturbators (probably including themselves) were neurasthenic. They therefore had to postulate a constitutional inferiority in order to explain why only some masturbators had problems. The problem pounders were inferior to begin with. It would be decades before masturbation was seen as incidental to the development of the so-called perversions and other problems, and not as the cause.

Sigmund Freud's 1905 *Three Contributions to the Theory of Sex,* or *Three Essays on Sexuality*, depending on the translator, first recognized the normality of the sexual instinct in children. While this may be taken for granted by today's reader, it was an extreme departure from the Victorian fantasy of childhood purity, and it caused shock and scandal in its time. While Freud acknowledged the existence of infantile masturbation during the nursing period (displaced pleasure from the mouth to other areas of skin), the fourth year (inquisitiveness and primacy of the phallus), and puberty (sexual tension), he firmly believed that "copulation is the normal sexual aim." Infantile sexuality terminated as perversion, neurosis, or a normal sex life. Masturbation after puberty was therefore perverse or neurotic.[20]

It was left to Freud's psychoanalytic followers to shift the prevailing view away from the notion that masturbation was the cause of neurosis or neurosis itself. Some continued to believe that masturbation might still be a symptom of unconscious problems that would require more psychoanalysis to resolve.

Psychoanalyst Wilhelm Stekel's *Autoeroticism* was published in German in 1917 but not translated into English until 1950. Stekel disagreed with his teacher, Freud, and saw masturbation as a universal and normal stage in development, believing that interference with this normal function caused the problems and was the basis "of guilty conscience. . . . What would be the present condition of the human race if that 'awful habit' were actually as harmful as our busy-bodies and ignorant meddlers have tried to make out?"[21]

Stekel described a continuum of "sexual acts carried out without the cooperation of another person" from the "cryptic onanism" or "larval onanism" of sexual fantasy, through the "masked onanism" of scratching, lip-smacking, and nose-boring, to the true "onanism" of masturbation itself. "Masturbation owes its highest pleasure-value to the fact that it is something forbidden."[22] It is a statement of personal power and control. "Every masturbator is Autotheos"—his own god. The more that the desire for self-gratification is repressed, then the more that desire grows. Stekel believed that without interference and the instillation of a guilt that enhanced both ambivalence and subsequent pleasure, the masturbator would give up the behavior on his own. For some adults, however, masturbation could be a useful defense mechanism as "asocial and cruel instincts [such as child molestation or homosexuality] may be expressed in the fantasy of masturbation." According to Stekel, the failure to exercise that defense could cause problems with violence in society or could cause an increased need to punish the self in the extreme consequence of suicide. Masturbation was not a "neurotic" but a "normal" sexual act.

Psycholanalyst Otto Fenichel wrote a paper, "On Masturbation" in 1938 but, like Stekel's work, it was not translated into English until 1954. Masturbation was considered normal for infants, children, and adolescents, and for adults "if it occurs only occasionally and in the absence of a suitable object."[23] Like Stekel, Fenichel believed that masturbation was not the cause of damage but a symptom of it. It could indicate immediate flight from tension, fantasy associated with introversion, or, if accompanied by anxiety and a bad conscience, neurasthenia. The old words and ideas had a life of their own.

The major contribution of psychoanalysis was not in its theoretical formulation, but in its recognition of the universality of sexual expression and the necessity to talk about it. The discovery of germs had ended physical degeneracy theory and the discovery of testosterone had terminated vital fluid theory. Psychodynamic formulations sounded the death knell for mental degeneracy theories. If there were problems associated with masturbation, they were individual in nature and there were no universal disorders.

By 1950 psychologist Albert Ellis could write in *Sex and the Single Male* that "masturbation leads to dissatisfaction, depression, and remorse [only] when one does not wholeheartedly accept it as a good and beneficial act, and when one erroneously believes that it is not satisfying."[24] "At times" some people get more gratification and satisfaction from masturbation than from sexual intercourse. "It is difficult to conceive of a more beneficial, harmless, tension-

reducing human act than masturbation that is sponta-
neously performed without (puritanically inculcated and
groundlessly held) fears and anxieties."[25]

In its 1972 publication, *Human Sexuality*, the American
Medical Association (AMA) declared masturbation to be
normal. "Regardless of how often it is practiced, it is neither
physically nor mentally harmful. Although it may produce
some feelings of guilt, masturbation is a normal part of adolescent sexual development and requires no medical management."[26] The AMA suggested that high sexual tension in
adolescents reminded parents of their own sexual tension
at that age and encouraged genuine parent-child communication about the phenomenon. There was no similar ringing
endorsement of adult masturbation; however, studies were
quoted which indicated a better sexual adjustment for those
who had masturbated.

The evolving view is that masturbation saves time and
money, avoids unpleasant alliances, is good for prostatic
health, and prevents sexually transmitted diseases. It prevents crimes, perversions, and serious mental breakdowns
and preserves family and social structure. As R. E. L. Masters said in 1967, if masturbation didn't exist, we'd have to
invent it. He wanted to call it "a different kind of pleasure"
rather than "second best."[27] To quote psychiatrist R. D.
Laing, the "solitude of masturbation can give the individual
the opportunity to discover what his position 'really' is and
what his desires 'really' are. For some individuals, masturbation can be the most honest act of their lives."[28]

As with religious writing about masturbation, medical
writing has evolved and been reflective of the times in
which it was penned. It has truly been part of the "social
constructionist" process. Only the conservative, traditional,
backward-looking "experts" refer to the ancient texts; however, like sin, the physical-and-mental-sickness model
doesn't seem to go away. For at least the last twenty-five
years, the medical message has been that we are normal.

It's time we moved beyond what we were taught to the contrary and accepted ourselves as we are, without hairy palms, acne, blindness, or mental illness.

NOTES

1. As quoted by John Money, *The Destroying Angel* (Amherst, N. Y.: Prometheus Books, 1985), p. 50.

2. Samuel A. D. Tissot, *A Treatise on the Diseases Produced by Onanism* (New York: Collins & Hannay, 1832), p. 17.

3. Ibid., p. 28.

4. Ibid., p. 45.

5. Benjamin Rush, *Medical Inquiries and Observations upon the Diseases of the Mind* (Philadelphia: Griggs & Elliot, 1812), p. 31.

6. Ibid., p. 345.

7. For more about these men, see Money, *The Destroying Angel*, chap. 2.

8. Ibid., p. 91ff.

9. F. R. Sturgis, "Treatment of Masturbation," in *Sexual Self-Stimulation,* ed. by R. E. L. Masters (Los Angeles: Sherbourne Press, 1967), pp. 32–51.

10. Hoag Levins, *American Sex Machines* (Holbrook, Mass.: Adams Media Corp., 1996).

11. Donald Greydanus and Barbara Geller, "Masturbation: Historic Perspective," *New York State Journal of Medicine* 80 (1980): 1892–96.

12. Henry Maudsley, *Pathology of the Mind* (New York: D. Appleton & Co., 1880), p. 452.

13. Ibid., p. 460.

14. Sturgis, "Treatment of Masturbation," p. 40.

15. Richard von Krafft-Ebing, *Psychopathia Sexualis* (New York: Stein & Day, 1886), pp. 189–90.

16. Havelock Ellis, *Studies in the Psychology of Sex,* vol. 1 (Philadelphia: F. A. Davis, 1900), p. 250.

17. Ibid., p. 259.

18. Ibid., p. 261.

19. Ibid., p. 282.

20. Sigmund Freud, *Three Contributions to the Theory of Sex* (London: Hogarth Press, 1905).

21. Wilhelm Stekel, *Autoeroticism* (London: Liveright, 1950).

22. Ibid., p. 197.

23. Otto Fenichel, "On Masturbation," in *Sexual Self-Stimulation*, p. 177.

24. Albert Ellis, *Sex and the Single Male* (New York: Lyle Stuart, 1950), p. 29.

25. Ibid., p. 32.

26. American Medical Association, *Human Sexuality.* (Chicago: AMA, 1972), p. 40.

27. R. E. L. Masters, "Introduction," in *Sexual Self-Stimulation*.

28. R. D. Laing, "Masturbation" in *Sexual Self-Stimulation*, p. 160.

Chapter Eight

———————■———————

Look in the Book[1]

———————■———————

The prime example of the evolution of the educational approach to masturbation in the United States is that publication which most of us turned to right after we put down our *Modern Home Medical Advisor*. Since it was first published in 1910, the *Boy Scout Handbook* has sold thirty-seven million copies in eleven editions. Boys were looking for the answers to their questions about personal development, citizenship training, and physical fitness. It has frequently been said that only the Bible has been read by more people. Actually, the Bible has never been copyrighted, so exact distribution figures are unknown and both *The Guinness Book of World Records* (eighty million) and Dr. Spock's *Baby and Child Care* (forty-three million) have outsold the handbook. Guinness lists no sexual records as official research teams don't seem to attend these events. Dr. Spock can't avoid the subject and is basically masturbation-positive for kids. Although he wanders into unresolved Oedipal gobbledygook, he basically advocates a low-key approach to parental concerns. The current *Boy Scout Handbook* is silent about masturbation. It wasn't always that way.

The founder of Scouting, General Sir Robert S. S. Baden-Powell, felt very strongly about development from boyhood to manhood. In *Rovering to Success*, a book for teenagers first published in 1927 and never revised during his lifetime, Baden-Powell indicated that there were certain rocks which one had to avoid as one paddled his canoe down the river of life. These rocks were horses, wine, women, cuckoos and humbugs, and irreligion. We'll pass on gambling, drugs, false prophets, and godlessness, and look at sex. Lessons about "women" included chivalry toward the weaker sex, avoidance of loose women, and conservation of the sex fluid, a substance vital to emerging manhood. Wasting it resulted in a weak heart and lunacy.[2]

This lesson may have been suitable for teenagers, but in 1908 the publisher of *Scouting for Boys* apparently thought that this would be too much for younger boys. Baden-Powell's original draft was never published. It read in part:

> You all know what it is to have at times a pleasant feeling in your private parts, and there comes an inclination to work it up with your hand or otherwise. It is especially likely to happen when you see a dirty picture or hear dirty stories and jokes.
>
> Well, lots of fellows from not knowing any better please themselves in this way until it becomes a sort of habit with them which they cannot get out of. Yet I am sure that every sensible boy, if he were told in time of the danger of it, would have strength of mind not to do it. . . .
>
> And the result of the self-abuse is always,—mind you, always—that the boy after a time becomes weak and nervous and shy, he gets headaches and probably palpitation of the heart, and if he still carries it on too far he very often goes out of his mind and becomes an idiot.
>
> A very large number of lunatics in our asylums have made themselves mad by indulging in this vice although at one time they were sensible cheery boys like any of you.
>
> The use of your parts is not to play with when you are

a boy, but to enable you to get children when you are grown up and married. But if you misuse them while young you will not be able to use them when you are a man; they will not work then.

Remember too that several awful diseases come from this indulgence—one especially that rots away the inside of men's mouths, their noses, and eyes, etc.

Baden-Powell's second draft was equally unacceptable:

Continence

Dangers of Self-Indulgence and How to Avoid Them.

These points are gone into in a separate paper which will be forwarded to anyone applying for the same and enclosing one penny stamp.

In a letter to his publisher, Baden-Powell lamented that "the promotion of continence is one of the main reasons for starting the scheme [of Scouting]; and letters which I have from some high authorities encourage me to think that it is perhaps the most important of the whole lot."[3]

The strength of Baden-Powell's convictions may have come from several sources. He paraphrased the then-popular Victorian semen theory of sexuality that would have appealed to him given his military background: One had been issued only a limited number of rounds (sperm for pro-creation) and one should not waste them. He also reversed the cause and effect relationship of idiocy and public mas-turbation. Baden-Powell glorified self-control, a trait thought by some to be a prerequisite for taking orders unquestioningly and thereby being a good soldier for the empire. However strong the convictions, the publisher was unmoved and the material was not printed. It did not cross the Atlantic, either.

The first American edition of the *Handbook*, published in

1910, forcefully stated, under the heading of "continence," that "for an instructor to let his boys walk on this exceedingly thin ice without giving them a warning word owing to some prudish sentimentality, would be little short of a crime." That was the entire discussion.

It was not a coincidence that Baden-Powell's words prevailed in the literature of the Boy Scouts of America. Two other individuals who had been instrumental in the founding of Scouting in the United States also had boys' organizations; however, the handbooks of Ernest Thompson Seton's Woodcraft League and Daniel Carter Beard's Sons of Daniel Boone focused solely on outdoor skills and not on sexual morality.

Some early Boy Scout leaders were remarkable in their quest for moral principles. The first and only "chief Scout librarian," Franklin K. Mathiews, launched a campaign against literature that would "blow out the boy's brains."[5] These books were the dime novels that promoted adventure and not morality. Purity in literature and purity in body were not strange bedfellows in the organization. James E. West, the first chief Scout executive, was said to have been firmly rooted in Victorian principles of purity and chivalry.

When the first all-American edition was published in 1911, "continence" gave way to "conservation," a topic having nothing to do with the management of soil and water but with other natural resources. At puberty (this word has never actually appeared in the *Handbook*) the "sex fluid" entered the blood and brought "tone to muscles, power to brain, and strength to nerves. . . . Any habit which a boy has that may cause that fluid to be discharged from the body tends to weaken his strength, make him less able to resist disease, lower his ideals in life, and often unfortunately fastens upon him habits which later in life he cannot break."[6] Readers who wanted more information were referred to Dr. Winfield Scott Hall's book *From Youth into*

Manhood. This remarkable little book was published by the YMCA Press in eighteen editions between 1909 and 1927. Dr. Hall minced no words: "Departure from sexual right-living usually takes one or the other of two forms: first the so-called 'secret sin,' masturbation or self-abuse; and the second, improper relations with the opposite sex." Self-abuse "as the reader probably knows, . . . consists in the rubbing or moving of the penis with the hand, or causing friction in any other way which leads to an excited feeling." This is an unnatural act and,

> whenever we disobey the laws of Nature, we are compelled by Nature to suffer a penalty. There is no escape from Nature's penalty. . . . Nature punishes him by removing, step by step, his manhood.
>
> As this act is repeated from week to week, or as in some extreme cases, every day or two, the youth feels the foundations of his manhood undermined. He notes that his muscles are becoming more and more flabby; that his back is weak; his eyes after a time become sunken and 'fishy,' his hands clammy; he is unable to look anyone straight in the eye. As the youth becomes conscious of his weakness, he loses confidence, refuses to take part in athletic sports; avoids the company of his young women friends; and becomes a non-entity in the athletic and social life of the community.
>
> So far as his school record is concerned, he may succeed very well in his studies for a number of years but eventually his memory begins to fail, and just at the time when he is trying to prepare for some useful life work, he wakes up to the realization that his mind is as flabby as his muscles, lacking in force, originality, and the power to think things out.[7]

Hall erroneously believed that nocturnal emissions did not contain sperm so that they simply represented the natural relief of pressure in the seminal vesicles. This would be the normal outcome if the temptation to resist unnatural emissions were exercised via cold baths, walks, work, and light meals. Hall didn't know about testosterone and still believed in constitutional weakness or neurasthenia.

The specific *Handbook* reference to Hall's book ended in 1927 but its influence was obvious for another twenty years. Nocturnal emissions were a "perfectly normal experience," however, "no steps should be taken to excite seminal emissions. This is masturbation. It's a bad habit. It should be fought against. . . . Keep control of yourself in sex matters. It's the manly thing to do. It's important for your life, your happiness, your efficiency, and the whole human race as well."[8] Recommendations included keeping in training, a cold hip bath fifteen minutes before going to bed, and "advice from wise, clean, strong men."

After 1948, readers of the fifth edition had to search for sexually oriented material in a paragraph in the section entitled "Examination by the Doctor":

> Suppose you are worried because you have "wet dreams" or have practiced masturbation once in a while. If this happens, don't let it scare you. If it's a habit, break it! Sure it takes courage and the best way is to keep busy with lots of work and play. But talk it over with your doctor; just open up to him and let him set you straight.[9]

The 1959 edition was authored by William Hillcourt. He attempted a less judgmental approach in discussing "From Boy to Man." After the obligatory indication that wet dreams were "perfectly natural and healthy," he continued:

> There are boys who do not let nature have its own way with them but cause emissions themselves. This may do no physical harm but may cause them to worry. If anything like this worries you, this is not unusual—just about all boys have the same problem. Seek the correct answer to any question which bothers you about your development from boy to

man. Be sure to get your information from reliable sources—
your parents, your physician, your religious advisor.

Any real boy knows that anything that causes him to
worry should be avoided or overcome. It will help you if
you throw yourself into a vigorous game, work at an
absorbing hobby, strive to live up to your own high ideals.

Here, Scouting is your ally, as you try to live up to the
tenth point of the Scout Law, "A Scout is Clean."[10]

Before his death in 1992, Hillcourt stated, "I did not use
the word 'masturbation' in the text because it would not be
in the vocabulary of an 11 year-old." The 1965 edition (the
seventh) dropped the last two paragraphs of the previous
version, not for propriety, but in order "to make the number
of type lines fit page 425."[11]

In 1972 the American Medical Association declared
masturbation to be normal. Coincidentally, that same year
there was a major change in the Scouting program em-
phasis and a new edition of the *Handbook* was required.
The new authors wanted to keep current and to take a stand
on masturbation. The first printing of the eighth edition
included this paragraph:

> Many young men like to masturbate. This is rubbing the
> penis. People used to think this would cause weakness,
> insanity, and other physical and mental problems. Doctors
> today agree that it doesn't cause any of these and is really
> a part of growing up sexually.[12]

The Roman Catholic and Mormon churches (remember
them?) are major sponsors of Scouting units and their
approval of the new *Handbook* was needed. It was their
view that the sex education of adolescent boys was the
responsibility of parents, church, and the medical profession. Consequently, twenty-five thousand copies of that
printing were taken to the landfill. (At least they were not

symbolically burned.) The newer version simply stated: "You may have questions about sexual matters such as nocturnal emissions (also called 'wet dreams,') masturbation, and even those strange feelings you may have. Talk them over with your parents and/or spiritual advisor or doctor."[13] The "strange feelings" are never described more specifically. Arousal, perhaps?

The 1979 edition was again authored by Hillcourt; however, there would be no slip-ups this time. The text of "From Boy to Man" was "developed by a special 'national task force' based on a six-month period of seeking advice from all the main religious denominations."[14] After a brief description of puberty (the word is still not used) the *Handbook* continues, "While all this is going on you may be wondering what is happening to you. You may have strong feelings that you never had before. There are so many questions you would like to have answered." Six months of work and the committee managed to change "strange feelings" to "strong feelings." At least they didn't refer the reader to Hall's book for the answers to the questions. The reader is warned not to seek advice from friends and is referred to "parent, family head, religious leader, family doctor, or trained health advisor."[15] That list should not have offended Catholics, Mormons, foster parents, or Christian Science practitioners, so the task force probably felt that it had done a good job. Hillcourt did manage to be more specific a few pages later when he discussed, in a straightforward manner, the dangers of sexually transmitted diseases and teenage pregnancy and he suggested, "You owe it to yourself to learn what is right. Proper sex education will give you the knowledge you need. It will enrich your life."[16]

The authors of the tenth edition in 1990 and the eleventh in 1998 did not wrestle with puberty or masturbation. They left them out. The new section on "Sexual Responsibility" exhorts the reader to practice abstinence until marriage so as not to father unwanted children or contact diseases. He must also report abuse by child molesters.[17]

The *Boy Scout Handbook* has been a major force in the education and socialization of American youth for ninety years, but it has been unable to deal comfortably with the topic of sexuality. Its views have reflected the biases of contemporary religious and medical beliefs true to social constructionism and, if doubts or conflicts arose, the matter has been settled with conservative vagueness by the editorial board or simply cut out by the publisher. If the latest edition is a silent portent of the future, then the one-fifth of American boys who currently look to the *Handbook* for information and guidance will get no answer there.

The *Girl Scout Handbook* has never mentioned masturbation. The 1917 edition of *How Girls Can Help Their Country*, the first handbook written by Juliette Gordon Low, said only that "a Girl Scout keeps herself pure in thought, word, and deed."[18] The concept of "purity" must have been confusing, because the 1920 edition changed that word to "clean" and defined it as "keep[ing] body and mind free from the slightest familiarity or doubtful stain."

It also stated that: "It is a safe rule for a Girl Scout not to read things nor discuss things nor do things that could not be read nor discussed nor done by a patrol all together."[19] It was hoped that girls in 1920 understood what that meant. Reference was made to being especially clean during menstruation. This was part of a section entitled "The Health Guardian" and it exhorted a girl to stand tall, take exercise, rest and conserve energy, and supply her daily need for air, sun, water, and food as well as to keep clean. This was deleted in the 1933 revision.

Except for ongoing references to standing tall and eating a good breakfast, "Good Health in Action" did not reappear until current editions. The *Cadette Girl Scout Handbook* now notes that "sexual thoughts and daydreams are common" during "puberty" and suggests the familiar "talking with someone you trust, recording your feelings in a journal [or] cultivating a hobby or special interest." It also recommends abstinence as protection against unwanted pregnancy, sexually transmitted diseases, and AIDS.[20]

Both national Scout groups continue their long-established pattern of following rather than leading change in social constructs. Since 1998 "abstinence" education has been the law of the land if states want to accept federal money for sex education. This fear-based curriculum emphasizes the potentially horrible consequences and exhorts teens to abstain from "sexual intercourse," "sexual activity," or "genital activity," depending on the individual state's definition of "abstinence." While no one denies the value of abstention, one must also be realistic and consider alternative measures to prevent pregnancy and sexually transmitted diseases for that two-thirds of American teens who do not abstain from sexual intercourse.

NOTES

1. An earlier version of this chapter appeared as Edward Rowan, "Masturbation According to the *Boy Scout Handbook*," *Journal of Sex Education and Therapy* 15 (1989): 77–81.

2. Robert S. S. Baden-Powell, *Rovering to Success* (London: Pearson, 1927).

3. As quoted by Michael Rosenthal, *The Character Factory* (New York: Pantheon, 1986), pp. 187–88.

4. Boy Scouts of America, *Official Manual* (New York: Doubleday, 1910), p. 49.

5. Franklin Mathiews, "Blowing Out the Boy's Brain," *Outlook*, November 18, 1914.

6. Boy Scouts of America, *Handbook for Boys* (1911), p. 232.

7. Winfield Scott Hall, *From Youth into Manhood* (New York: YMCA Press, 1910).

8. Boy Scouts of America, *Boy Scout Handbook*, 1st rev. ed. (1938), p. 528.

9. Boy Scouts of America, *Handbook for Boys*, 5th ed. (1951), p. 412.

10. Boy Scouts of America, *Boy Scout Handbook*, 6th ed. (1959), p. 425.

11. William Hillcourt, personal communication.

12. Boy Scouts of America, *Scout Handbook*, 8th ed. rejected printing (1972), p. 334.

13. Boy Scouts of America, *Scout Handbook*, 8th ed. as printed (1972), p. 334.

14. Hillcourt, personal communication.

15. Boy Scouts of America, *Official Boy Scout Handbook*, 9th ed. (1979), p. 516.

16. Ibid, p. 526.

17. Boy Scouts of America, *The Boy Scout Handbook*, 11th ed. (1998), p. 376.

18. Juliette Gordon Low, *How Girls Can Help Their Country* (New York: Girl Scout National Headquarters, 1917), p. 8.

19. Girl Scouts, Inc., *Scouting for Girls* (1920), p. 12.

20. Girl Scouts of the U.S.A., *Cadette Girl Scout Handbook* (1995), pp. 60–64.

Chapter Nine

∎

Fantasy

∎

S ome of those Scouts sitting around the campfire were dreaming about their Indian and pioneer heritage and the heroes on the Norman Rockwell cover of their *Handbook*: Teddy Roosevelt, Charles Lindbergh, Abe Lincoln, and George Washington. Some were dreaming about selfless acts of chivalry, whether stopping runaway horses or blasting off on a mission to the moon and beyond. But most of them were probably fantasizing about girls: They found the lost Girl Scouts, lit a fire by rubbing sticks together in order to warm their shivering bodies, snared animals and gathered roots and berries to sustain them, and finally, led them to safety. They also snuggled together in sleeping bags and explored unknown delights as the grateful girls allowed anything and everything to happen. Well, that was my fantasy anyway. Other men have different fantasies.

Paul, the scoutmaster to whom I referred in the introduction, was imagining his scouts without uniforms and naked around the campfire. His fantasy was that the winner of a game got to sleep in the same bag with him

141

and he measured achievement not in the number of merit badges but in the number of times one got to perform oral sex on the leader. He clings to that fantasy in prison because it is the opposite of his current "wife" status.

Stan has a fantasy about little girls. He played doctor when he was about eight and his vision of people hasn't changed much since. At least twice a day he masturbates to the fantasy of a girl he calls Jane. She has an eight-year-old face on a mature woman's body, the latter courtesy of *Playboy*. They may have sex or may just talk about their children. Jane is an imaginary companion to a man with very limited social skills.

As an adolescent, Sam had fantasies about a classmate. He wrote her name on his penis with hair tonic and then whacked away. Although he never had a relationship with her, he has noted that the women he has been attracted to as adults bear a resemblance to her and that most of his fantasy women do, too.

Lynn daydreams about the perfect partner. He may be someone from the daytime soaps or someone she has met socially. They may have dinner or dance or just talk. This leads up to a very romantic seduction. If the scene has been particularly arousing, she will masturbate.

Gary came into therapy because he couldn't control his spending on phone-sex calls. He needed guidance in his fantasy and concrete directions to arousing images while he masturbated.

Fantasy and masturbation go hand in hand, so to speak. Not only is it difficult to masturbate to an empty mind, but it also feels good to finish an arousing fantasy with a good orgasm. Fantasy and masturbation become mutually reinforcing. A review of what we know about fantasy, then, is important to an understanding of why we masturbate.

Granted, this is a male perspective: Alfred Kinsey found that 89 percent of men fantasized while masturbating but only 64 percent of women did. Thirty-six percent of women focused on the sensation alone when masturbating.[1]

Everyone fantasizes at some time. Everyone has sexual fantasies. While it seems to be almost unequivocally accepted that the occurrence of sexual fantasy, per se, is normal, an assessment of the content and a value judgment of that fantasy might result in more diverse interpretations. In one view, the psychoanalytic, Freudian sexual fantasy, like the masturbation usually associated with it, is always an expression of "neurosis" or other underlying pathology.

In another view, fantasy is the inherent human faculty to interpret life's events and guide future action. This neurophysiologic perspective suggests that the brain activity characteristic of REM (Rapid Eye Movement) sleep, dreaming, and fantasy simply reflects a higher evolutionary plane of development, the ability to plan ahead. I think, therefore, I fantasize.

A third interpretation is a behavioral one. If I fantasize (with or without masturbation), attend to the sensation, experience pleasure, and assign it positive value, then I become more comfortable and involved, like it more, and do it more.

Am I a stimulus-response automaton, a thinking animal, or a seething cauldron of unconscious hostility? Probably a little of each of the above.

In addition to these formulations, there are other important variables in fantasy patterns. Far and away, the most important is gender. Men and women have very different fantasies. To a lesser extent, age (experience) and intelligence (creativity) are also important. Fantasy also depends on its social and cultural context for form and content.

The question as to whether or not "anatomy is destiny" will be debated for the rest of our lives, or as long as the

Holy Grail of politically correct androgyny is pursued. Nevertheless, it is quite clear that a person with a protruding, external penis thinks differently about sexuality than does a person with a hidden, internal vagina.

Many researchers, including psychologist Robert May, have compared men and women in their interpretations of an ambiguous picture (Thematic Apperception Test, or TAT) or other fantasy productions, and described clear differences.[2] Feminine themes are characterized as internal, expressive, caring, nurturing, and focused on inner, emotional life and relationships. Masculine themes are external, instrumental, prideful, and controlling. Men win and women live happily ever after. In May's study, one picture was that of a man on a trapeze about to catch a woman flying toward him. In a typical female story, the couple had overcome difficulties in their relationship and were now going on to stardom together. In a masculine story, she was screwing the sword-swallower, so he dropped her. Such a pattern of interpretation is already established by adolescence.

Obviously, there is more to fantasy than half the population thinking like an erect penis. There is a complex interaction among the effects of different bodies, different gender caregivers, and different cultural roles in the evolution of masculine and feminine thinking and fantasy patterns. The analysts focus on the evolving sexual relationship with that primary infant caregiver, the mother. For both sexes, mother changes from the source of all nourishment and comfort of omnipotent infancy to the great "no-sayer" of childhood. As part of the great potty battle, the message was that whatever was under the diaper was dirty: "Keep your hands off!" Perhaps it is easier for girls to accept this and to identify with mother, but boys have a thing that sticks out and they soon take pride in learning to do tricks with it while simultaneously coming to the realization that it is bad. As Nancy Friday so colorfully put it, "He stands self-convicted: a dirty animal reveling in his sexuality, angry and forlorn in the knowledge that it is unacceptable to women."[3] Not only is sexuality unacceptable to mother, it is also unacceptable to the objects of his early adolescent sexual desire. The girls have identified with mother. It's dirty down there—and besides, they are thinking in terms of relationships, not sexual activity.

The scene is set. In this view, masculine fantasy is infantile and takes revenge on women for the sexual suppression of childhood and the sexual withholding of adolescence. For Robert Stoller, the basic dynamic of fantasy was hostility. Fantasies are "memorials raised to commemorate painful experiences and relationships of infancy and childhood plus, as life proceeds, endless alteration of the script for maximal effectiveness. The function of fantasy is to convert these painful experiences to pleasure while still keeping the details of the earlier traumas and frustrations embedded in the fantasy, to allow an endless repetition that reverses trauma to triumph."[4] The alterations are created in order to avoid indifference and/or boredom, and they include risks, secrets, and built-in safety factors, while the underlying tension (hostility) leads to greater excitement and drama. It also means that the one who fantasizes does not have to act out that triumph in the real world. The happy ending of a triumphant fantasy is best celebrated by orgasm.

Some analysts, like Stoller, believe that there is only one basic story line (also called the scenario or script) and that it is based on fact. Psychiatrist N. Lukianowicz thought that individuals remain faithful to a masturbatory pattern throughout life and that it "always represents the true object of desire." He based his conclusions on the fantasies of "imaginary sexual partners" of 188 patients who had sought treatment because they thought that they masturbated too much. (This has to be a biased sample because I've personally never had a man seek help with this complaint.) Some of these patients were very psychotic. Lukianowicz likened the imaginary partners to the imaginary playmates of "solitary and emotionally isolated individuals." One case study in this report is that of an 18-year-old who was depressed because he thought that his brain had dried up as a result of "self-abuse." "A frank discussion of the matter and a few ECTs [electric shocks] helped to free him from his fears and feelings of guilt."[5] You bet: Punishment relieves guilt. To generalize from this population of patients to the world of men at large is absurd.

Friday called male fantasy "the triumph of love over rage" and she believed that it gives a good picture of the unconscious mind of the person who invented it. She does appear to be more open to the concept of a metaphor of real or imagined trauma rather than a literal rendition as its basis, however. In her view, the theme of male fantasy is that whatever the man does, it has been suggested or initiated by the woman who took responsibility for it and who was then totally grateful, supportive, and forgiving.

Let's not get stuck in what some might consider the psychobabble explanation of fantasy, however. A behavioral explanation based on repetition of what feels good or a neural model based on rehearsing possible paths of thought could be equally valid.

Very little is known about the sexual fantasies of children. Psychologists Steven and Ruth Gold and Robert Bauserman asked college students to recall earlier fantasies. Gold and Gold found that males recalled fantasy at an earlier age than did females and that male fantasy was briefer, more positive, and more sexually explicit than that of females.[6] Bauserman found that prior to age twelve, students had romantic fantasies, not specifically sexual interactions, and they were limited to a child's knowledge of sexuality. Fantasy partners were classmates and unknown older persons. If there were specific images, then they were drawn from television or magazines, and more so in males than in females. Adolescents had more boyfriend and girlfriend fantasy and more specific sexual acts were included. It is of interest that Bauserman found that in many childhood fantasies reported by adolescent girls, there was no partner.[7]

Adolescence is a time of self-definition in identity, vocation, sexuality, intimacy, and values: Who am I? Is that okay? What will I be when I grow up? How do I get laid? Do I need anybody? What do I stand for? Fantasy is an integral part of the process of definition, but it is complicated by the adolescent male urge to respond to erections. The forward-looking penis is seeking relief, not relationship. The adolescent female is looking to inner experiences such as the start of menses, emotional investment, and romance. For girls, sex is equated with love and commitment; for boys it is a defiant step toward freedom. Love comes later. The boys keep secrets from parents, try to be with the guys jerking off and looking at pictures together, and create lives of their own. No wonder there is such a mismatch as one group seeks autonomy and the other group seeks interpersonal competence.

Adolescent male fantasy tends to be organ oriented and free of the strings that real teenage girls attach to sex. Friday's "virgins" fantasized wild young women who didn't need much stimulation to achieve orgasm; mild, ignorant young women who thought that everything was wonderful; and permission-giving older women who took responsibility. This couples a macho image with childlike performance anxiety.

Nancy Friday wrote two books about female sexual fantasy, *My Secret Garden* in 1973 and *Forbidden Flowers* in 1975. For the first book, she requested female fantasies in ads in newspapers and magazines. The second book contained fantasies sent in by readers of the first. No attempt was made to define the demographics of the first four-hundred-plus sample other than to note that the average age of respondents who gave their age was twenty-two. Every woman in the sample masturbated and each one fantasized during masturbation. Friday suggested a number of different reasons for female masturbation, including such diverse motivators as frustration, exploration, and pure daydreaming. Friday also divided the themes into "sixteen rooms in the house of fantasy."[8]

At the end of *Forbidden Flowers*, Friday asked her male readers to send in their fantasies. Three thousand did. Another one thousand responded to a request in a column in an unidentified men's magazine. Keeping in mind all that we have said about sampling in the area of sexuality, we must accept the data from *Men in Love* with reservations about generalizing it to the whole population. Keep in mind also, that, for Friday, anger toward women is the driving force in male fantasy. That might suggest a bias on the part of an author who attributed no universal dynamic to female fantasy and went out of her way to make no value judgments on the fantasies of her female respondents.

While women had preferred vague, anonymous strangers in their fantasies, the men were much clearer in their object choices. For Friday's men, the fantasy women were sexually insatiable. Unlike mothers and rejecting adolescent girls, the fantasy women loved them for whatever they did sexually. Male scenes included oral sex both as recipient and giver, anal sex, incest, fetishes, cross-dressing, sadomasochism, lesbian sex, and groups. No woman in Friday's books had fantasized anal sex, fetishes, sadomasochism, or observation of gay men together. For the men, female permission was critical, yet autonomy and control were never really lost. If two women were having sex, the man didn't have to choose, yet everyone was satisfied. If he shared his woman with another man, she approved and he did not have to acknowledge any homoerotic fantasy. If there were groups, then they were small with rarely more than four people, and a majority of women gave not only more variety but also more permission.

Morton Hunt discovered a great deal about sexual fantasy. Three-quarters of his men fantasized having intercourse with a loved one or acquaintance, and one-half with a stranger; however, the latter was frequently someone known from books, magazines, or movies. One-third fantasized having sex with more than one woman at a time, 19 percent did things they wouldn't do in reality, 13 percent forced someone to have sex, 10 percent were forced to have sex, and 7 percent had sex with another man. Comparable figures for women were that four-fifths fantasized sex with someone they knew, one-fifth with strangers, one-fifth with more than one man, 28 percent did things they wouldn't do in reality, 19 percent were forced to have sex, 3 percent forced someone to have sex, and 11 percent had sex with another woman.[9] Obviously, many people had more than one kind of fantasy.

Many researchers have looked at the question of force in female sexual fantasy. Early thinkers (mostly male) had speculated that such fantasy was associated with guilt or a secret desire to be sexually assaulted. Several studies have found female fantasy more associated with daydreaming (77 percent) than with masturbation or intercourse (33 percent) and correlated with sexual experience and arousability, not with guilt.[10] Psychologists David Strassberg and Lisa Lockerd found that half of their undergraduate women had fantasized about "forced sex," but the woman was not hurt, the man was attractive as a lover, and the woman was really in control. Again, these women had more sexual experience, more fantasy, and less sexual guilt than those who did not fantasize.[11]

Males are quite visual in their fantasy orientation. This is as consistent with the idea of looking forward and externally as it is with the influence of testosterone on the visual cortex during fetal development. Perhaps men are more concrete and need to see a picture while women are more abstract. Many women get really excited by romantic novels where the relationship with the mysterious stranger is the key element. Many men discard them saying, "Nothing happened." Part of male bonding may be a sharing of images. I wonder how many guys jerked off to the same pictures: Gibson girls, Vargas girls, Marilyn Monroe calendars, Farah Fawcett and Kristy McNichol posters, Madonna on MTV or Pamela Anderson on *Baywatch*. Pictures may be more tangible and "real," less threatening, and more arousing than internally generated fantasies. Vividness is correlated with degree of arousal. This begs the question of a comparison of male and female fantasies in terms of color, action, and clarity of the actors and themes. There's a research project out there for someone—but please, use a population other than undergraduate introductory psychology students.

So far, we have avoided the word "pornography," whatever that is. Mr. Justice Potter Stewart once said, "I shall not today attempt to define [it], . . . but I know it when I see it. . . ."[12] That is actually an accurate definition, as one man's porn is another man's yawn. Many men create their own erotic material based on their own fantasies. This may be their own drawings or incidental material such as the now-defunct Sears catalog. (Was that why gramp spent so much time in the outhouse?) Commercial pornography caters to preexisting patterns; it does not create them. In sex shops, devotees find "golden showers" and "big, milky tits" in different bins, and there is an equally wide range of XXX Web sites. Different strokes for different folks. Edward Laumann noted that pornography is repetitious; he thought it indicated that the erotic imagination is limited. In his widely quoted 1991 work, Danish researcher Berl Kuchinsky found that less than 3 percent of Danish pornography was "highly deviant" and he found no relationship between the increased availability of violent pornography with the incidence of rape in the United States, Denmark, Sweden, and West Germany from 1964 to 1984.[13] It has even been argued that access to pornography actually decreases the incidence of sex crimes. In 1970 the U.S. Commission on Pornography had found the material to be harmless. Cloaked in moral indignity, President Nixon refused to accept the report.

Although it may be the literature read with one hand, pornography does not drive men to act out their sexual fantasies. Fantasy itself is almost always harmless. The only exceptions are those individuals whose fantasy pattern is described as "paraphilic." These men (the condition is rare to nonexistent in women) demonstrate an obsessive, driven quality to fantasy that cannot be resolved except by acting out the fantasized behavior. They commonly report that masturbation doesn't relieve their tension; they have to do the deed. Ron's fantasy image, described in chapter 1, is quite clearly one of prepubescent girls without pubic hair or breast development. Even though he masturbated to that image, it didn't go away. He repeatedly sought out little girls to fondle. That's why he's in prison. Here again, it is not the fantasy per se that is the problem, it is the underlying dynamic of the sexual arousal. Most studies show that fewer than 5 percent of sex offenders fall into this pattern. The vast majority of sex offenders are predatory opportunists and the criminal dynamic is one of power, not sex.

So what about the hostility, rage, anger, and power that are supposed to be the basis for all sexual fantasy? Good question. Neither your fantasies nor mine are hostile, are they? Just ask us. Unfortunately, we are not the best judges of that because we probably don't understand the unconscious dynamics of our own thinking patterns. It is just because these dynamics are unconscious and often metaphorical that it is not an issue for most of us. Our infantile and juvenile anger has been tempered by experience with intimate relationships. We have learned that supportive, permission-giving, loving people who accept our sexuality do exist and that these feelings can be reciprocal. Experience tells us that our needs can be met given the right circumstances.

Remember, too, the concept of psychic causality: Nothing happens without a reason. We may be afraid of heights because it was scary looking over the top of the crib when we were two. We may not like spinach because it was the "green ice cream" in the central battle of the great "clean-plate club" war at age five. We may avoid medical care because mother said that if we didn't stop talking and go to sleep, she would take us to the doctor for a shot. Are these experiences really different from putting down blondes because of that cute girl in the fifth grade who didn't give us a Valentine after we spent a dollar on hers, or because of that lady next door who sunbathed in the nude but never asked us over for cookies and an afternoon in bed?

One finding common to many surveys is that there is a small decrease in sexual fantasy as we get older. Sustained intimacy and support may have overcome some earlier needs, but shit still happens and we still need to fantasize triumph. Another interesting finding is a subtle shift toward the adoption of opposite gender roles after midlife. Women become more prideful and controlling and men more concerned with inner experience and whole-body sensation. Obviously, this can be beneficial to both. Fantasy reflects these changes.

We have already made reference to the fact that preadolescent children of both sexes, and a significant number of adolescent girls and postadolescent women, masturbate not to visual fantasy, but to feeling. Adolescent and postadolescent males turn outward to focus on accomplishing the task of ejaculation, and they no longer experience the inner, sensuous feelings leading up to it. For men, a scripted fantasy helps to achieve the goal, for, as one man told Friday, "Masturbation without fantasy would be too lonely." For women, a scriptless or sensory style fantasy is the journey itself. This latter use of the term "fantasy" then, becomes multisensory and multimodal and suggests a much broader range of input. It is not an "empty mind."

The depth of involvement with the sensual process or, alternatively, the ability to become absorbed in that process, is the basis for the absorption theory proposed by Don Mosher in 1980. This is a feeling theory, not a thinking theory. The depth of absorption is correlated with the degree of arousal and, in fact, the relationship is one of mutual feedback as more arousal leads to more absorption, leading to more arousal and so on.[14] The process is hindered if one is stuck in a script. While such a structured thinking pattern might initially help to focus on arousal, it ultimately interferes with letting go of thoughts and of allowing sensation to assume primary importance.

What does this matter to the pumpers and pullers and pounders? Nothing, if their goal is only in the coming; but it matters a great deal if they hope to rediscover the underlying process of sensuality and sexuality and to determine where they got off the track. Some may recognize these concepts as sharing commonality with altered states of consciousness, self-hypnosis, meditation, and Tantric yoga. While these may have different philosophical bases, they share in the suspension of goal-directed behavior and in attention to the journey. For our purposes, total attention, absorption, hypnotizability, altered states of consciousness, sexual trance, and meditative or Tantric state are equivalent. It's where we are, not where we're going or where we've been. The idea of masturbation as meditation is not a new one to Eastern philosophy or to women.[15] To many men, though, it sounds like that romance novel where nothing happens.

Fantasy represents different things to different people. It is more than an expression of neurophysiologic connections and not necessarily a dynamic formulation of repressed hostility. It can be an anticipation of future encounters or a safe rehearsal of potential interactions. It may satisfy a need for variety in activity and/or partners without having to act on it. It could introduce forbidden or "bad" images into mental life or function as a safety valve to discharge them. Fantasy can increase arousal for masturbation or for sex with a partner. One can share fantasies for increased play potential. A fantasy can be a dependable plot or the introduction to variety. In fantasy, one can be completely narcissistic and not be concerned with a partner's pleasure or with fear of judging or being judged on performance. It may represent an inner form of power and help to define individual identity. It may also be a sexual vision quest or pure escapism. Fantasy, like masturbation, is inherently a value-free act.

Why, then, is fantasy a secret? If basic sexual behavior is shameful, then fantasizing about it is as bad, or worse. The more powerful, violent, or deviant the fantasy, the more likely it is to be viewed negatively. Fantasy and masturbation go together. The concepts of "larval onanism" and "the occasion of sin" are still very much with us. We tend not to broadcast our feelings of shame and guilt. One of the real benefits of sharing fantasies and feelings would be the discovery that lots of guys want Madonna to sit on their face and then write a song about how wonderful it was. It has nothing to do with that Valentine in the fifth grade. Really.

NOTES

1. Alfred Kinsey, Wardell Pomeroy, Clyde Martin, et al., *Sexual Behavior in the Human Female* (Philadelphia: W. B. Saunders, 1953), p. 667.

2. Robert May, *Sex and Fantasy* (New York: W. W. Norton, 1980).

3. Nancy Friday, *Men in Love* (New York: Laurel, 1980).

4. Robert Stoller, *Sexual Excitement: Dynamics of Erotic Life* (New York: Pantheon, 1979), p. 30.

5. N. Lukianowicz, "Imaginary Sexual Partners and Visual Masturbatory Fantasies," *Archives of General Psychiatry* 3 (1960): 429–49.

6. Steven Gold and Ruth Gold, "Gender Differences in First Sexual Fantasies," *Journal of Sex Education and Therapy* 17 (1991): 207–16.

7. Robert Bauserman, "Fantasy in Childhood and Adolescence: An Exploratory Study," paper presented at the annual meeting of the Society for the Scientific Study of Sexuality, Chicago, 1993.

8. Nancy Friday, *My Secret Garden: Women's Sexual Fantasies* (New York: Pocket Books, 1973).

9. Morton Hunt, *Sexual Behavior in the 1970s* (Chicago: Playboy Press, 1974), p. 92.

10. J. Kenneth Davidson and Linda Hoffman, "Sexual Fantasies and Sexual Satisfaction: An Empirical Analysis of Erotic Thought," *Journal of Sex Research* 22 (1986): 184–205.

11. Donald Strassberg and Lisa Lockerd, "Force in Women's Sexual Fantasies," *Archives of Sexual Behavior* 27 (1998): 403–14.

12. *Jacobellis* v. *Ohio* 378 U.S. 184 at 197.

13. Berl Kuchinsky, "Pornography and Rape: Theory and Practice?" *International Journal of Law and Psychiatry* 14 (1991): 47–64.

14. Don Mosher, "Three Dimensions of Depth of Involvement in Human Sexual Response," *Journal of Sex Research* 16 (1980): 1–42.

15. Margo Woods, *Masturbation, Tantra and Self Love* (San Diego: Omphaloskepsis Press, 1981).

Chapter Ten

———— ■ ————

Man versus Woman

———— ■ ————

Sex is like bridge. You need a good partner or a good hand. Let's talk about the partner. For this discussion we will focus on heterosexual couples.[1]

We have already seen that there are many, many differences between men and women with regard to sexuality. The primary difference, of course, is sex in the context of feelings and relationships rather than sex as an expression of power and control. In the last chapter, we looked at differences in fantasy, "pornography," and absorption in inner process. Previously, we looked at statistics about masturbation. Despite the apparent liberalization of our society, a smaller percentage of women masturbates. While that percentage has clearly grown over the years, it still does not approach the near-universality of male masturbation. There has been a significant change in that today's women are masturbating at a younger age and with higher frequency than did their mothers. One extremely significant piece of data is the very high percentage of women who are not orgasmic during sexual intercourse. Reliable textbooks give that figure a range from 10 to 90 percent, with a bias toward higher figures.[2] This would suggest that one of the main reasons for women to masturbate is to have an orgasm.

Another real difference between men and women with regard to sexuality is the willingness of the latter to be more open to self-discovery. Women know that they don't know and they are willing to learn. Men don't know that they don't know and don't think that there is anything that they need to learn. That might be an overgeneralization, but remember, men rarely stop and ask for directions when driving, either.

In addition to countless women's magazine articles stressing the right to orgasm, there have been several good books promoting sexual enhancement for women. These range from the gentle, pink-covered, step-wise, "preorgasmic" program of *Becoming Orgasmic* by Julia Heiman and Joseph LoPiccolo,[3] to *For Yourself* by Lonnie Barbach,[4] to the original "Ladies, kick-start your vibrators," *Liberating Masturbation*,[5] and its follow-up, *Self-Loving*, by Betty Dodson.[6] *Becoming Orgasmic* has a companion set of teaching tapes for home use, *For Yourself* has a *Discovering Orgasm Workbook*, and Dodson's books are based on her body-sex groups for women. Women gather in a circle observing, practicing and sharing thoughts and techniques, and talking about their emerging sexuality. Listen up guys, there's something to learn here. Bernie Zilbergeld's *Male Sexuality* in 1978[7] and *New Male Sexuality* in 1992,[8] and the *Celebrate the Self* magazine are the masculine equivalents of these do-it-yourself manuals. My suspicion is, however, that men have not sought out these books on their own but have had them recommended by lovers, friends, and therapists.

As a group, men appear to avoid reading about sexuality (as opposed to reading about "sex") and talking about it with women. They especially don't talk to women about masturbation, and more especially, don't talk to their partners about it. To be fair, women don't talk to men about masturbation much either.

In the *Kinsey Institute New Report on Sex*, June Reinisch quoted the study of a group of twenty-four heterosexual couples without sexual complaints. The unidentified researcher found that all forty-eight individuals were masturbating in addition to having sexual intercourse with their partners, and not one person knew that his or her partner was masturbating.[9] This should not be surprising, given the frequency of masturbation for the first finding and the frequency of poor communication for the second. In the 1940s, Kinsey had found that 40 percent of married men and one-third of married women masturbated an average of once a month. In the 1970s, Hunt found that 72 percent of men in committed relationships masturbated an average of twenty-four times per year, while 68 percent of women in committed relationships masturbated about once a month. Hunt suggested that this did not mean that 1970s partners were less satisfying but that masturbation as an alternative rather than as a substitute was more acceptable for both sexes.[10]

Poor communication about marital masturbation is the norm. Recent articles in *Redbook* and *New Woman* asked the provocative questions: "Is it normal for a man to masturbate when he's involved in a relationship?" and "Does your husband masturbate?"[11] The answer to both, of course, was "Yes." If one had been schooled only in the "natural" view of marital sex, then the coexistence of intercourse and masturbation would indicate the possibility of a problem in the relationship and the certainty of a problem in the masturbator. It ain't necessarily so.

Kim brought her husband to "therapy" because she had walked into the bathroom one evening and found him reading *Hustler* and masturbating. She was devastated. They had been married only a few months, made passionate love almost every night, and she thought herself to be an attractive woman. Ken agreed completely. Kim was beautiful and sexy and lovemaking was wonderful. He felt aroused whenever she was around but he also wanted time for himself. He liked to fantasize that he was attractive to the models in the magazines. He had always masturbated. Happily for this couple, they were willing to read and to talk about their feelings and differences. Kim accepted that Ken was normal and that her response was normal, too. Her discomfort did not go away completely, however, and the issue may very well reappear at a time when she is particularly vulnerable. Late in pregnancy with a resultant poor self-image and fatigue might be such a time.

We have already reviewed the general reasons for masturbation, and they certainly apply within the context of a marriage or any other committed relationship. There is usually a grudging acceptance that the absence of a partner, physically or psychologically, might be a justification for masturbation.

Ray, the retired physician, knows that his wife of forty years still wants to be close to him, but she hasn't been interested in sex since menopause. He suggested estrogen replacement but did not pursue the issue when she declined. Mary says that she feels intimate but sex is not important. Ray masturbates at least twice a week but feels lonely every time. He thinks that Mary knows, but he doesn't want to talk to her about it because he fears her scorn. He accepts that he is normal but he thinks that he avoids a confrontation by remaining silent.

Ruth is a sixty-six-year-old widow. Whenever she sees a travelogue about Hawaii, she is reminded of the wonderful time she had there with her husband many years ago. She may then masturbate with thoughts of Jim and the way he used to touch her. Sometimes she thinks she ought to feel guilty, but that thought passes quickly. It's a good feeling and a good memory.

Chronic illness and indifference are often cited as reasons for masturbation as the only source of orgasm within a marriage. For some individuals, the enforced separation of military assignment or incarceration makes it easier to masturbate rather than to engage in potentially risky relationships. Recall however, that the most commonly cited reason for masturbation in Hunt's survey was tension reduction, sexual or otherwise.[12] The added tension of arousal followed by the release of orgasm produces general relaxation. A person would not have to involve or inconvenience anyone else and relaxation could be achieved reliably and efficiently. No one would feel used. Comfort too, could be achieved without imposition on another person who might have neither the time nor the inclination to comfort.

Some men and women in committed relationships have sex with a partner and then masturbate afterward. This may represent freedom to fantasize without having to share that fantasy or the freedom to self-pleasure at will. The potential for more intense orgasms, a higher sex drive, and the reassurance that arousal and orgasm are still possible even when inadequately achieved with the partner are possible explanations as well. For men, the need to be in a better position to win the "sperm wars" is instinctive and not conscious. Let's also not forget those women who are not orgasmic with intercourse and need to masturbate in order to relieve their sexual tension.

So why not just speak up? "Excuse me, Martha, I'm uptight so I'm going into the can and jerk off." "Back in a few minutes, Grace, I can't sleep so I'm gonna put a tape in the VCR and pump 'til I come." "Sorry, Jim, I've had a hard day. I'm going to take a warm bath and get off." "Enjoy the meeting, Butch; I think I'll go to bed and take care of myself." Shame and guilt about masturbation are still the main reasons for not speaking up, but the relationship itself adds another dimension. We might keep the need for masturbation from our partner for fear that he or she might feel inadequate, or less altruistically, because we might feel inadequate ourselves for not having sex with our partner and know that he or she is dissatisfied. A feared, and often realized, response to the discovery of partner masturbation is anger.

> When Sally found Pete masturbating in front of the late movie, her first response was to call him a "pervert" and a "pig." Pete oinked and felt ashamed. She carried on about his "mental adultery" in fantasizing having sex with the women on the screen. "What's wrong with me?" she wailed. In therapy, Sally talked about her feelings of abandonment and rejection. Clearly they were long-standing issues for her but they were intensified by her discovery. Pete was finally able to reassure her that he had no thoughts of infidelity and that theirs was an exclusive sexual relationship. He saw masturbation as an independent option in addition to marital sex. Sally is reassured about fidelity but unconvinced about the options. Pete is still demonstrating the former and working on the latter.

Let me hasten to point out that this is not an unequivocal endorsement of marital masturbation. Not every reason is appropriate. There are explanations as to why one or both partners masturbate that clearly point to problems in one or both individuals and/or in the relationship itself. Obvious individual problems include both compulsive masturbation and specific sexual dysfunctions which exclude the partner.

> Jeff masturbated several times each day: in the car on the way home, in the bathroom, and in the garage. Sally felt that he had no time for her and that she must be unattractive. The more she pressed him, the more he masturbated away from her.

> Tim had problems getting an erection except when he masturbated, so he avoided intimacy with Carol for fear of

failure. She tried to act more seductively but Tim felt even more threatened and masturbated even more.

Jeff and Sally and Tim and Carol are examples of couples who become involved in what is called a "pursuer/distancer" relationship. One aspect of this may be that as one partner (usually the wife) pursues sexual intimacy, the other (usually the husband) distances himself by masturbation. Both feel victimized: one uncared-for and the other nagged. The sexual behavior has to be addressed within the larger context of the relationship dynamics.[13]

A preexisting pattern of masturbation may also carry over into the martial relationship.

> George was a rigid guy. When he was single he had masturbated to a scenario where he made love to a passive woman who followed all his directions including being tied to the bed and he wanted Paula to do the same. For George she was a new and exciting instrument of his fantasy. Paula felt restricted and controlled and asserted her right to be herself. The relationship did not survive.

We need to consider why a partner might be unavailable or if personal or relationship dynamics play a role. Possible individual reasons include severe depression, anorexia, post-operative or post-partum body changes with resultant poor self-image, or stress and the resultant lack of interest in sex. The interpersonal dynamics of withholding marital sex may be quite complex and go beyond simple anger and avoidance. Withdrawal, punishment, revenge, insecurity, and passivity might potentially play a role. Individuals or couples experiencing these dynamics might consider psychotherapy in order to deal with the issues involved.

> After Tommy was born, Rose felt overwhelmed in caring for the newborn and the last thing she wanted was Big Tom pawing her body. She told him to do it by himself.

Bill was chronically depressed and how low sexual desire.
Marti masturbated in order to relax in what she perceived
to be a very tense household.

Another perspective on the communication problem in
male-female relationships is found in *That's Not What I
Meant* and *You Don't Understand*, where linguist Deborah
Tannen discusses the linguistic cultural differences between
men and women.[14] Her basic premise that women commu-
nicate for involvement and men for independence is certainly consistent with the gender differences in sexual
behavior that we have already discussed. Feminine communication patterns are described in terms such as sensitivity,
inclusion, involvement, rapport talk, symmetry, connection,
affiliation, and consensus; while masculine patterns are
assertive, hierarchical, performance oriented, report talk,
asymmetrical, ordered, and aggressive. Girls interact with
girls and women with women in ways different than boys
interact with boys and men with men. When gender differences are framed in those cross-cultural terms, then they are
perhaps easier to understand and accept. Good people who
truly love each other can still think and act differently.

Tannen's reference to linguist Gregory Bateson's concept of "complementary schismogenesis," a mutually aggra-
vating spiral of escalating conflictual behavior, sounds exactly like the pursuer/distancer relationship. Partners may
genuinely want to interact positively, but each keeps doing
more of what the other did not understand in the first place,
and communications worsen. Written by a woman in feminine linguistic style, these books are not the "how-to" manuals a man might have written. Tannen does suggest that
insight, followed by conscious awareness of one's own
interactional style, acceptance of difference and avoidance
of blame, practicing the other's style, and, finally, choosing
to interact in the other gender's style without habitually
reverting to one's own, will improve communication.

When it comes to masturbation, it would be helpful to consider it in this perspective. Masturbation in the context of a relationship, marital or otherwise, is an extension of the individual thinking and behavior that preceded that relationship. The challenge is to incorporate it, as well as all the rest of our individual thoughts and behaviors, into complex interactions with another person. The process could be speeded up considerably by talking about it and sharing information about our communication styles and our sexuality. Partners can masturbate themselves together. Not only may this represent a turn-on for both, but it can also be a powerful learning experience. Demonstration is the best teaching technique. The ability to maintain eye contact may actually promote a higher frequency of mutual orgasms and one can also learn a wider range of erogenous zones. Introducing a toy may mobilize both conflict (competition) and cooperation. Mutual masturbation (of each other) could be the next step and might even include the introduction of a vibrator into partner sex. It shouldn't come as a surprise that some sex manuals recommend partnered masturbation.[15]

We don't talk to the adults we love, and we don't talk to our kids about sex. Silence causes confusion. Kids do hear about masturbation. They can easily find websites for wankers (See Appendix). Billy Joel can sing that "Captain Jack will get you high tonight" and the Divinyls sing "I touch myself." "Icicle" by Tori Amos, "Longview" by Green Day, and "Mastabata" by Adam Sandler also touch on the subject. Films such as *There's Something About Mary*, *The Truth About Cats and Dogs*, *Pleasantville*, *Spanking the Monkey*, and *Even Cowgirls Get the Blues* also include masturbation. *Seinfeld* and *Roseanne* had episodes about it. Rockers simulate masturbation in music videos and on stage, but some of these messages are ambivalent at best about the normality and natural function of masturbation. We need to teach that it is even more than that. For instance, if adolescent males were encouraged to masturbate using condoms, they would become accustomed to that feeling and not hesitate to keep partner sex safe. But first, they have to be encouraged to masturbate.

> Nick and Bette tried to be very open with their six-year-old and to answer her questions about sex. The message was that it was perfectly normal to touch herself and to masturbate. When Jean started doing it at the dinner table, Nick said simply, "That's for private places."

While that may be as good as it gets in the real world, there is still an undercurrent of shame that a precocious child would recognize. The open promotion of masturbation is still a liberal utopian concept and not part of a religiously conservative utopia at all. Sociologist John Gagnon found that fewer than half of the parents surveyed about sex education wanted their children to have a positive attitude toward masturbation although a large majority knew that their children were masturbating.[16] Not only does this complicate future adult communications, but, it also makes it extremely difficult to counsel someone that they ought to be masturbating.

NOTES

1. Men with male partners are discussed by David McWhirter and Andrew Mattison in *The Male Couple: How Relationships Develop* (Englewood Cliffs, N.J.: Prentice Hall, 1984). Women with female partners are discussed by Margaret Nichols in "Lesbian Relationships: Implications for the Study of Sexuality and Gender," in *Homosexuality/Heterosexuality: Concepts of Sexual Orientation*, ed. David McWhirter, Stephanie Sanders, and June Reinisch (New York: Oxford University Press, 1990), pp. 350–66; and Karlein Schreurs, "Sexuality in Lesbian Couples: Implications for the Study of Sexuality and Gender," *Annual Review of Sex Research* 4(1993): 49–66.

2. Sandra Leiblum and Raymond Rosen, eds. *Principles and Practice of Sex Therapy*, (New York: Guilford, 1989), p. 54.

3. Julia Heiman and Joseph LoPiccolo, *Becoming Orgasmic: A Sexual Growth Program for Women*, 2d ed. (Englewood Cliffs, N.J.: Prentice-Hall, 1984).

4. Lonnie Barbach, *For Yourself: The Fulfillment of Female Sexuality* (New York: Doubleday, 1975).

5. Betty Dodson, *Liberating Masturbation* (Self-published, 1974).

6. Betty Dodson, *Sex for One: The Joy of Self-Loving* (New York: Harmony Books, 1987).

7. Bernie Zilbergeld, *Male Sexuality* (New York: Bantam, 1978).

8. Bernie Zilbergeld, *The New Male Sexuality* (New York: Bantam, 1992).

9. June Reinisch, *The Kinsey Institute New Report on Sex* (New York: St. Martin's Press, 1990).

10. Morton Hunt, *Sexual Behavior in the 1970s* (Chicago: Playboy Press, 1974). See p. 86 for comparison with Kinsey.

11. Frank Pittman, "Solitary Pleasures," *New Woman,* March 1992, p. 116; Neil Chesanow, "A Touchy Subject," *Redbook* [circa January 1992], p. 94.

12. See chapter 4, p. 66.

13. Stephen Betchen, "Male Masturbation as a Vehicle for the Pursuer/Distancer Relationship in Marriage," *Journal of Sex and Marital Therapy* 17(1991): 269–78.

14. Deborah Tannen, *That's Not What I Meant* (New York: Ballantine, 1986), and *You Just Don't Understand* (New York: Ballantine, 1990).

15. Cathy Winks and Anne Seamans, *The New Good Vibrations Guide to Sex*, 2d ed. (San Francisco: Cleis Press, 1997).

16. John Gagnon, "Attitudes and Responses of Parents to Preadolescent Masturbation," *Archives of Sexual Behavior* 14 (1985): 451–66.

Chapter Eleven

———————————— ■ ————————————

My Own
Worst Enemy

———————————— ■ ————————————

W hen a man engages in a power struggle with his penis, the penis invariably wins. An oppositional vagina is another sure winner. With the penis or vagina in control, there may be disorders of desire, lubrication, erection, and/or orgasm/ejaculation; however, there are now therapeutic programs or sex therapy interventions to help a person make peace with that vagina or penis and to work cooperatively with it in order to resolve their conflicts.

"Sex therapy" refers to the specialized treatment of sexual dysfunctions with a combination of talk and exercises. William Masters and Virginia Johnson pioneered the treatment of sexual difficulties with their first major work on the subject, *Human Sexual Inadequacy* in 1970, a work addressed to the scientific community.[1] Writers Fred Beliveau and Lin Richler's *Understanding Human Sexual Inadequacy* was published later that same year and popularized Masters and Johnson's work by providing a simple-language version for the general public.[2]

In the beginning, heterosexual couples went to acknowledged sex therapy experts in specialized treatment centers for help: Masters and Johnson in St. Louis, William Hartman and Marilyn Fithian in Long Beach, or Helen Singer Kaplan in New York City. These centers trained other therapists and, over time, sex therapy evolved using a variety of formats to treat not only heterosexual couples, but singles, gay men and lesbians, and groups, as well.

Along with advances in the development of a scientific approach to sexual dysfunction, advances were also made in the education of the public. Sexual self-help books have become best-sellers. As previously noted, some of the better ones for women are *Becoming Orgasmic, For Yourself,* and *Sex for One.* They encourage "preorgasmic" women to masturbate as part of a program leading to sexual fulfillment.

As the sex therapy field has grown more sophisticated, it has come to embrace everything from recommended reading to prescribed exercises to intensive psychotherapy. A simple yet extremely useful formulation to help explain the variety of treatment interventions is Jack Annon's sequential model of sex therapy, the **PLISSIT** model.[3] The sequence is:

> **P**ermission
> **L**imited **I**nformation
> **S**pecific **S**uggestions
> **I**ntensive **T**herapy

Permission to acknowledge ones own sexuality, to read about it, to experiment with it, and to talk about it with a partner, friend, or therapist can be a wonderfully freeing experience. Permission to exchange simple communications can make a real difference. One of the most common comments heard in couple's therapy is, "He (or she) never told me that." Simple messages such as, "Don't be so rough, it turns me off," or "I'm tired at night and prefer to make love in the morning" can make a world of difference. Permission to be open and to think and talk about sexuality may lead to reassurance, correction of misunderstandings or misconceptions, or the filling of gaps in sexual knowledge.

Limited information from the literature can be helpful in the process of education or correction in filling the discovered gaps: "Married men commonly masturbate." "Older men need more direct stimulation for erections than do teenagers." "Certain medicines for high blood pressure can interfere with performance." "Many women have rape fantasies." "There are no calories in semen." Simple facts can relieve guilt or anxiety or provide the basis for further discussion.

Specific suggestions are derived from the information found in the professional or self-help literature or from therapists: "If there is poor partner satisfaction, consider these other techniques. . . ." "If there is a focus on performance, try to relax and forget the goal." "If there is poor muscle control, do Kegel exercises." "If anorgasmic, follow these steps for better results." No problem is perfectly unique. Someone has dealt with it before and written about the results.

Finally, *intensive therapy* addresses underlying conflicts and past history as part of individual or group psychotherapy, or it provides an individually tailored educational and/or behavioral program for those who have been unsuccessful at previous levels of intervention. At this level, therapists seek to uncover and resolve the negative feelings associated with sexual pleasure. These may be a fear of intimacy, a power conflict, or an unresolved past physical and/or mental trauma. Behavioral programs at this level might include systematic desensitization or shaping exercises.

It follows from this model that some people will do just fine with the permission, limited information, or specific suggestions found in self-help books. Others will not and they should seek assistance. Some need to hear the basic information from a professional who thus awards a higher standard of permission to the advice. Others recognize that they do not have the motivation, discipline, or understanding to change themselves and they turn to a sex therapist for help.

What is a sex therapist? Ideally, he or she is a professional with a medical and/or social service background, such as a psychiatrist, psychologist, social worker, or psychiatric nurse practitioner, and has an interest and training in dealing with problems in sexuality. Most states do not regulate "sex therapists" as such, and, as a result, there are no legal restrictions on using that term. Notes that are tacked up on street-corner bulletin boards or ads in personal columns that offer "sex therapy" suggest that, in these instances, the term is equivalent to "escort service" and related to a different profession. How, then, does one find a legitimate therapist? Physicians and psychotherapists often know colleagues who specialize in the field of sexuality. The American Association of Sex Educators, Counselors, and Therapists (AASECT) has certified therapists since 1968 and publishes a directory.[4] Certified therapists are required to have academic degrees, course work and seminars, high ethical standards, and extensive supervision. A person so certified can be expected to display a reasonable standard of competence. It is also appropriate to ask a potential therapist for his or her credentials. These should include licensure or certification by a state board of registration that regulates that particular professional discipline.

As sex therapy has evolved over the last thirty years, masturbation has continued to be viewed as an integral part of treatment. There are specific situations in which masturbation is helpful, if not essential, in overcoming disorders experienced in the phases of desire, excitement, and orgasm. For most of us, masturbation was basic training for later sexual experiences. The bottom line, therefore, is that if a dysfunction was learned with masturbation, then the best way to treat or "unlearn" it is with masturbation. Masturbation also allows a person to learn about his sexuality without the complications of interpersonal relationships or special equipment.

As we review the various sex therapy approaches at each phase of dysfunction, we will provide general outlines, but we will focus on the role of masturbation in treatment. Almost by definition, then, this chapter is addressed primarily to men. Women don't seem to masturbate dysfunctionally. As a tool for self-acceptance, exploration, and becoming orgasmic, masturbation exercises for women are described in the next chapter.

Disorders of Desire

Sexual desire is primarily psychological in origin in that it is cognitively or emotionally inspired. All of us develop our personal turn-ons over time. For a typical man during his adolescent and adult years, thousands of thoughts occur in association with orgasm. Many of these orgasms are obtained while masturbating. Behaviorally speaking, specific thoughts repeatedly reinforced by pleasurable orgasms become even more powerful stimuli in the future.

When a person's thoughts or opportunities do not lead to arousal, he is identified as having "low desire." This has always been a common female difficulty and it is becoming an increasingly common complaint in men referred for sex therapy. It is too simplistic and quite invalid to say that this is only a passive response to the power of the partner in relationships. A lack of interest in sex, or low or absent sexual desire, is not necessarily pathological. In circumstances of pain or fear, it would be logical to avoid arousal. Similarly, a depressed mood, a raging anger, the wrong partner, or high anxiety about performance could also explain a lack of desire. Low desire may represent a change from a usual pattern, be confined to specific situations and/or partners, or be associated with other factors such as taking a particular medication. This applies to masturbation as well as to partner sex.

> Fred is a fifty-five-year-old school principal who wasn't interested in sex. His wife, Carol complained because she felt unloved. Fred insisted that love was not the issue; he just didn't feel sexy any more. He did not even see it as a problem but reluctantly agreed to therapy because Carol insisted. A number of issues emerged. Fred felt impotent (his word) in school because he didn't agree with curriculum changes and was in conflict with his superintendent. Carol was quite happy in her job and liked to talk about it over dinner, to Fred's dismay. He acknowledged that he now drank too much and was depressed. He had also failed to achieve an erection on two occasions and didn't feel like trying and failing again.

This is a typical presentation, as low desire is usually psychologically determined, is often not in conscious awareness, and is "just the way I am." As such, it is also resistant to self-help and usually requires intensive therapy. With the therapist, a person would look for unconscious blocks to intimacy or success and he would identify conditions most favorable to arousal. If the conditions apply to masturbation as well as to sex with a partner, and "nothing turns me on, ever," then therapy might focus on an understanding of the absence or avoidance of all sexual pleasure. It might be necessary to trace the developmental pathway of adolescent fantasy in order to understand the blocks. Creative and arousing new fantasies might need to be discovered and then reinforced with orgasms. In Fred's case, the issues of job dissatisfaction, alcohol, depression, and avoidance had to be addressed directly, and Carol was actively involved in reestablishing conditions for relaxation and arousal.

Beth and Ursula, two of the women we met in chapter 1, provide examples of low sexual desire in women who have had no experience of sexuality associated with pleasure. Ursula grew up in a persistently sex-negative environment and never thought that sexual behavior could feel good. Because of childhood sexual abuse, Beth associated sexual feelings with trauma and pain and she not only avoided sexuality psychologically but she avoided it physically as well. One form that this physical avoidance can take is *vaginismus*, or the contracture of the vaginal musculature to prevent penetration. The dual-treatment approach of dealing with psychological avoidance in intensive therapy and with the physical response by mechanical stretching with fingers or surgical rods is beyond the scope of this book; but a logical first step, especially for women with a history of sexual abuse, is to make friends with the genitals and see them as beautiful rather than shameful. The empowerment of masturbation would be a positive next step in the process of becoming orgasmic.

If there is "deviant" male desire, the role of masturbation in therapy is clearer. The particular "wrong" turn-on has almost invariably been the subject of multiple masturbatory orgasmic reinforcements, that is, jerking off too many times to the wrong fantasies.

Three of the vignettes in chapter 1 referred to men with potentially problematic patterns of arousal and sexual desire. Tom liked to wear pantyhose and heels, Ron had to picture little girls, and Alex needed to watch his wife dress and undress in order to be "turned-on."

Each of these examples could be very different than it seems at first. What if part of Tom's turn-on included stealing nylons from clotheslines or bureau drawers? What if his wife helped him dress as part of their lovemaking? What if Ron fantasized about a little girl but knew that he would never act on his fantasy? What if Alex demanded that his wife change her hair style and dress to look like his sister? The critical point on the continuum of fantasy from normal to dangerous is the point at which it involves another nonconsenting person. An uncontrollable obsession that interferes with day-to-day function is equally problematic; however, it is more difficult to define that crossover point.

It is unusual for a man to identify a fantasy as dangerous before it is too late and he is already in trouble. For that rare man who sees potential danger, there may be benefit to a self-help approach based on the limited information of awareness and understanding of how the turn-on evolved and the specific suggestion to himself to "knock it off." This kind of insight is rare because the typical male (or female) has no frame of reference for arousal other than his or her own experience and it seems perfectly normal to be turned on by nylons, kids, or strippers. Only when an outsider defines the behavior as "deviant" does the person get the message that there is another standard and he doesn't fit in. For this reason, problem fantasies require intensive therapy.

Historically, there have been at least three ways to therapeutically decrease deviant arousal. One is by talking and developing insight.

> Tom: "When I was in third grade, I sat in the front row and the teacher's desk was on a raised platform. Mrs. Baker always wore nylons and heels and I stared at them for hours each day and dreamed about how wonderful they might feel."

> Alex: "I know that the turn-on from my wife's dressing and undressing is directly connected to doing the same with Sis."

No doubt this approach works with a few, but for the majority with deviant desire, insight through talk therapy is easier said than done. Besides, insight is not the same as change. The fantasy persists, the tension builds, and the force is beyond one's rational ability to control it.

A second, more extreme approach, is medication to take

away sexual fantasy. Thioridazine (Mellaril) is a powerful antipsychotic tranquilizer, and some men who take it report that it does reduce sexual fantasy. It also interferes with erection and can cause heavy sedation as well as many other side effects and, because of the possibility of retinal pigmentation, it might ultimately cause blindness. A much more specific drug is medroxyprogesterone acetate (Depo-Provera), an antiandrogen that reduces the level of testosterone, the hormone associated with a man's sexual desire. (Cyproterone acetate, a similarly acting drug, is available in Canada but not FDA-approved for use in the United States.) The major side effects are weight gain and strokes, but most men who take it report that they just don't think about little girls, or shoes, or any kind of sex anymore. This is a temporary solution for extreme situations and not a permanent one, unless, of course, one considers a stroke or blindness as a final solution in the prevention of acting out on sexual fantasies. While drugs may decrease fantasy, they do not change the content of the fantasy.

The third approach is a behavioral one. Such techniques start with simple ones like thought stopping by saying "Stop!" and focusing on another thought. Physically snapping a rubber band worn around the wrist or pinching oneself, or pairing a terrible smell (ammonia, for example) with each "bad" thought are slightly more complex, as is thinking of negative consequences like sitting in the drunk tank in those nylons and pantyhose.

Other behavioral approaches are based on the premise that one can relearn arousal in the same way that it was learned in the first place, by masturbating. Masturbating more to "good" fantasy and less to "bad" fantasy doesn't cause blindness or strokes the way that medicines can. This simple but elegant treatment plan was developed by psychiatrist Gene Abel. It is called "masturbatory satiation," and combines the critical elements of more good fantasy and less bad fantasy.[5] This is not a "do-it-yourself" solution, as it requires a therapist. The approach takes advantage of the refractory period, that time after an orgasm when it is not possible to get another erection or to ejaculate. A man first masturbates to orgasm to a "desirable" fantasy. After orgasm and pleasurable reinforcement of the "good" stimulus, the man then masturbates for an hour to his very favorite and most vivid "deviant" fantasies. In order to stay honest throughout the process, he tape records his ongoing fantasies while masturbating and then the therapist does random checks of the tapes to make sure that he stays on course. The therapist may also make suggestions about the content in order to enhance the effect. Ron, for example, would first masturbate to an increasingly detailed fantasy of making love to a consenting adult woman. (This could also be a man if the deviant fantasy objects are little boys and the gender orientation is homosexual.) After the orgasm, Ron would switch immediately to his images of little girls with as much detail as he could imagine and describe. He would include as many sights, sounds, smells, tastes, and touches as he could. One hour of beating a nonresponsive penis to a favorite fantasy can lead to pain, boredom, negative feelings, or all of the above. It works except in unusual cases where the refractory period is minimal and/or the preexisting pattern included several orgasms in a row. Researchers and therapists find this behavioral approach to be a very powerful one in the lab. Unfortunately, current research has shown that such reconditioning usually does not generalize beyond the lab.

Most current treatment programs fall within the so-called cognitive behavioral paradigm of understanding and acting differently. One has to learn to identify the cycle of offense and how the fantasy fits into that cycle. The goal is to prevent relapse, not prevent fantasy. The offender needs to separate fantasy from acting out on it. Talking about the fantasy should make it less intense as alternative behaviors are developed in order to control the stress that the fantasy had previously relieved. It is not even necessary to totally eliminate masturbation in this treatment program.

All of these examples refer to sex offenders as men. The very logical explanation for this is that it is quite rare to identify a female sex offender. A 1990 article about women who molest children found them to be mentally ill, developmentally disabled, and/or acting in the company of a dominant male pedophile.[6] I have heard a clinical history of one woman who appeared to fit the pattern of exclusive sexual arousal to children and she had been well-conditioned as a third-generation victim of maternal incest. Other than this one case, I know of no examples. The local papers have recently carried stories of three female teachers who had sexual relationships with students—two with boys and one with a girl. Without more clinical information about these individuals, it is impossible to make a diagnosis; however, even if all were true pedophiles, the condition would still be extremely rare in women and the treatment approach would be the same anyway.

PROBLEMS OF ERECTION/LUBRICATION

The worst sexual problem that most men can imagine is to be aroused but not be able to perform: "You're not a man if you can't get it up and keep it up." "There's nothing as humiliating as a limp dick." This happens to most men at some time in their lives and there is usually a perfectly good reason for it. The anxiety symptoms that follow failure perpetuate the problem. A failure creates the fear of failing again; a fear of failure produces anxiety in anticipation of that failure; anxious anticipation leads to observing detachment or spectatoring rather than to feeling participation.

Usually, the problem occurs when performing for someone else. Most men who do have difficulty with a partner do not have difficulty when they masturbate alone. In fact, an inability to get erections for masturbation or at any other time should trigger a medical evaluation to rule out physical causes of the problem.

Self-help programs are of some benefit in dealing with erectile failure, especially when the problem is a new one. Information about the real cause of the initial failure (when still remembered) and specific suggestions for exercises to promote relaxation and maximize conditions for good performance may be sufficient. A classic example is Jim's report: "I was out at a party and had a lot to drink when I picked up this beauty. It was late and I really wanted to impress her and to have sex with her. I couldn't get it up." No wonder, with alcohol, fatigue, and pressure to perform all lined up against him. However, "we just fell asleep and in the morning it all worked out fine. It was even better because we knew what we were doing." As a result, there was no long-standing problem. Ralph described a similar scenario with a woman he met at a bar, but "she laughed at me and walked out." He was worried about future performance. If he follows self-help instructions, Ralph might overcome the problem. He could recognize the cause of the failure and take off the pressure by trying to perform only in relaxing circumstances, but he might need more help.

There are many books that describe therapeutic steps with a partner. They work best when the partner reads them, too. When the couple establish conditions to only touch and feel good and not to worry about erections, then there is no pressure to perform, no anxiety, and no uninvolved spectator. When this is insufficient or partners cannot stick to the rules, intensive therapy may be needed. Often this simply restates the ground rules with formal prohibition of intercourse and the paradoxical suggestion to relax so that arousal can occur naturally. If these are not successful, then there is a search for the dynamics of noncompliance: "Why don't these folks go along with the program?" "What purpose does this problem serve in the relationship?" "Is there a function to the dysfunction?"

A man without a partner can work the program by masturbating. (Yes, there are surrogate partners if you live in California, but that's part of another culture.) Masturbatory rehearsal can be helpful even with a partner. Confidence in the erection and clarification of the turn-ons can enhance progress with another person. It is also helpful to confront the disaster of loss of erection by losing it deliberately and then gaining it back with masturbation. By taking control of the letting go, a man can then take control of bringing back the erection.

Psychologist Bernie Zilbergeld suggests adding a masturbatory fantasy of competence.[7] For a man without a partner and with a reluctance to establish a relationship for fear of failing sexually, this is probably the best technique for getting started. Instructions start with the fantasy of romantic buildup, seduction, and performance in a completely competent and confident manner. The basic principle is the maintenance of a relaxed, anxiety-free state in a wide variety of situations. If anxiety appears, then the visualization is changed to regain the relaxed state. It is important that over time, but not all in the same practice session, fantasies include all the possible variations and situations that might be encountered. These include visualization of potentially anxious situations, such as oral sex, penetration, or farts, and then relaxation again in the fantasy. The fantasy should include that ultimate dread, loss of erection. A man should visualize losing it, then relaxing, and then doing something to get erect again.

This program worked for Ralph. He was comfortable in masturbating and achieved good erections. He was able to relax and to get into his fantasies, including the worst-case scenario of being laughed at. He developed a positive fantasy response of "just kidding" and was able to regain the erection. Ralph also became aware that alcohol and fatigue were not positive conditions for his arousal. He was able to put his insight, visualization, and rehearsal together in order to make love successfully, and his confidence was restored.

Masturbatory fantasy reduces the anxiety about getting back into a relationship and it also provides a well-rehearsed alternative tape to play in the mind instead of observing performance in real life. In real life, as in fantasy practice, there should be a focus on the visualization of feeling competent rather than a retreat to the role of being a spectator to anxiety. As part of masturbatory training, it is important to pair ejaculations with full erections. While it is certainly possible to ejaculate with a less-than-rigid penis, it is poor learning and it could ultimately reinforce a less than fully satisfying pattern of sexual performance.

At this point, some readers must be wondering "Why does he go on about reconditioning when there are all these quick fixes for erectile dysfunction?" The answer is that I am troubled by the increased "medicalization" and "patholo-gizing" of sexuality. This begins with the premise that most dysfunction has an "organic" cause and requires an "organic" cure. If the cause is a medication side-effect, then, by all means, reassess that medication. If a person has advanced diabetes or neurological dysfunction, then treat that medically as well. If that does not resolve the erectile dysfunction, then consider medical intervention. However, if anxiety is the basis of the problem, consider alternatives to the quick fix. Granted, we want our current crises resolved in thirty minutes—less commercial breaks—but a solution to the problem that causes anxiety/conflict may be better.

There is a wide range of technologies available to the erection-challenged. Solutions include penile implants—either flexible or inflatable, depending on whether one wants Gumby or a water balloon sewn into the penis. Vacuum pumps placed over the flaccid penis are pumped, the penis engorges with blood in the vacuum, and then a rubber band is popped on to keep the blood from flowing out. Papaverine, phentolamine, and combinations of those can be injected directly into the penis. Alprostadil may be injected or delivered by pellet into the urethra. Sildenafil (Viagra) also does the job of relaxing corporal smooth muscle and producing an erection. Yohimbine is supposed to increase arousal. Supplemental testosterone should be prescribed only when the level is low. All of these drugs and devices require a prescription and are perfectly appropriate for problems with a true physical basis.

Men are not alone in the medical marketplace, as drug manufacturers have turned their attention to women as well. The concern is the same: conflict resolution versus symptomatic relief. This debate is just beginning as sildenafil is being prescribed for an increasing number of women with various sexual dysfunctions.

For women, vaginal lubrication occurs in the excitement phase, and dysfunction, a failure to lubricate, causes dryness. This results in "dyspareunia" or painful intercourse. According to psychologist Arnold Lazarus, half of these women are in unsatisfactory relationships and are simply not aroused.[8] Assuming that there is a high level of desire, a failure of physical arousal would suggest that the dryness was a result of hormonal changes such as estrogen depletion or medications such as antihistamines. This requires medical evaluation and change of therapy is appropriate. Some victims of childhood incest associate impending sexual contact with trauma and not with arousal. Other developmental factors such as very negative attitudes about sexuality might also produce fear, loathing, or anxiety rather than arousal. In such circumstances, sex therapy and/or intensive psychotherapy are the treatments of choice.

PROBLEMS IN EJACULATION/ORGASM

Along with problems in desire and erection, difficulties with ejaculation/orgasm are a major issue addressed by sex therapy. While the inability to achieve orgasm (anorgasmia) is a common complaint among women who seek sex therapy, it is relatively rare among men. Sandra's experience is a good example of programs available to "preorgasmic" women. Alone or in groups, women explore their bodies, touch themselves, learn to masturbate effectively, and are then able to share these techniques with a partner, if appropriate. The progression is simple and usually effective.

Occasionally, a man may never have ejaculated, either by masturbation or with a partner. Usually he is a socially isolated individual who has never figured out how to have an orgasm, is reluctant to get involved with a partner for fear of appearing really dumb, and is motivated for therapy because he feels that he is missing something. His lack of knowledge of how to come to orgasm can be dealt with by showing him a video about masturbation: See one, then do one. Instructions about masturbatory technique may be helpful, and once the ejaculation barrier is broken, the man can then be supported in learning the appropriate social skills in order to have a sexual relationship with a partner. For him, this is a normal developmental sequence that has been delayed. Even more rarely, a socially engaged, intellectually bright individual has never had an orgasm. If he cannot duplicate the video performance, then he should have a medical evaluation to rule out physical reasons for his inability to ejaculate. If the exam shows nothing, an intensive therapeutic approach is usually necessary because simple explanations to the problem are unlikely.

The failure to ejaculate with a partner in a man who is able to masturbate to orgasm is almost always an indication for intensive therapy. An exception to this rule is the adolescent for whom anxiety about first performance with a partner may block ejaculation. If this limited information and the suggestion to keep trying under less anxious circumstances are not sufficient, then he, too, is a candidate for therapy.

A couple may not even recognize that failure to ejaculate is a problem. If the man lasts long enough so that the woman is orgasmic and satisfied, she will not complain that he has not ejaculated. Besides that, the sheets stay dry. It is usually the desire for pregnancy that brings the issue to light. As part of an infertility work-up she undergoes all sorts of tests and his sperm is counted after he masturbates into a jar. Only after she is proven to ovulate and his sperm is proven to be viable does someone finally ask if these events occur in such a context as to promote fertilization. Does he come inside her during intercourse? Having gathered the critical piece of information that he does not, their physician then refers him for sex therapy.

The treatment approach requires both talk therapy and behavioral conditioning. The "symptom"—inability to ejaculate inside a partner—solves an emotional conflict. The underlying reasons may be simple, complex, rational, or weird, but are real nonetheless. If there is fear of pregnancy, reluctance to share intimacy, or an inability to let go of control, then it makes sense not to have an orgasm. If one is afraid that the ejaculation will drain vital essences and transfer magical power to the partner, or that teeth inside the vagina will bite off an offending, spitting penis, then it also makes sense (of sorts) not to ejaculate. Sometimes too, there may be a belief that ejaculation is an act of disloyalty to a deceased or divorced wife or to a live or dead mother, or a loss on one's slim hold on any sense of power in the relationship. The treatment approach differs according to the nature of the motivation.

The behavioral therapy technique used in the treatment of delayed ejaculation with a partner presumes successful masturbation, and then "shapes" the ejaculation through a series of successive approximations to ejaculation inside the vagina.

> Joe could masturbate to orgasm alone in the bathroom but not in bed with Cindy. Starting with what worked, Joe first masturbated in the bathroom with the door closed. He then proceeded to masturbation in the bathroom with the door open and Cindy watching. He then masturbated while sitting in a chair in the bedroom, then while sitting on the foot of the bed, and then lying next to Cindy. He either did it by himself or Cindy masturbated him. Then came the tricky part. Taking advantage of the principle of ejaculatory inevitability, Joe masturbated toward orgasm. When he felt the stirring in his pelvis and he knew that he was coming, Joe quickly inserted and ejaculated into the vagina.

This wasn't much fun for Cindy, but she knew that they were working on a specific problem, and she had previously been instructed in the mechanics. She accepted short-term frustration in the service of long-term pleasure and pregnancy. Joe was also stimulating her to orgasm on separate occasions throughout this behavior-modification period. If the timing were wrong and he could not ejaculate, Joe then withdrew and masturbated more until the point of inevitability again approached and he then tried another insertion. Following successful completion of that step, he tried to enter earlier in the sequence, realizing that, after a time, he might have to pull out and masturbate to the critical point, and then reenter. The final successful step was vaginal entry, thrusting, and ejaculation without masturbation. This program did not address any psychodynamic reasons for Joe's difficulty. Had the behavioral approach been unsuccessful, then intensive therapy would have been indicated.

Although this may seem like a tedious example, behavioral shaping could be used in other contexts as well. For instance, if one wanted to be orgasmic by nipple stimulation or fantasy alone, then one could focus on that stimulus or erotic thought to maximum arousal, masturbate to the brink of orgasm, and continue the stimulus or thought pattern. It is anticipated that hands-on genital stimulation would be progressively less necessary and that, eventually, the orgasm would be produced by erotic thought or other stimulation alone.

What about the worst-case scenario, where there is no history of ejaculation at all, even with masturbation, and a couple wants to get pregnant? We stress the pregnancy aspect again because a simple failure of the man to ejaculate when the woman is satisfied by orgasm doesn't seem to lead couples to treatment. A man who masturbates but cannot reach orgasm may use techniques that enhance or increase stimulation. Three common ones are the testicular squeeze, anal stimulation, and the Valsalva maneuver. As he masturbates toward a higher level of arousal, the man (or his partner) may reach down and gently squeeze his testicles or lightly stroke his anal opening. He may do the Valsalva by holding his breath and increasing pressure within his abdomen as if he were bearing down to force a bowel movement. One or a combination of these moves may push him over the threshold of stimulation necessary to trigger orgasm and ejaculation. If all of this does not work, and if talk therapy doesn't uncover any resistances, then one may simply have to acknowledge a treatment failure. Some therapists have had success with hypnosis at this point. If the goal is pregnancy, as it usually is, then a referral of the man for electrostimulation to produce the ejaculate and the sperm necessary for artificial insemination of the partner might be appropriate.

If difficulty in coming to ejaculation is potentially impossible to treat, then the opposite condition, premature ejaculation, is relatively easy to control. There is no equivalent condition in women. Control of premature ejaculation represents one of the real contributions of self-help sex therapy. This has been a mixed blessing for therapists as we no longer seem to have the very high success rate (90 to 95 percent) reported by the therapeutic pioneers. Many of our potential patients and clients read books and have slowed down by themselves using the techniques to be described. Those who do seek therapy may now have more complex problems.

> Graham was very upset when Bridget complained that he came too quickly. His first wife had never said anything about it. He had read that lasting a minute or so was average and he didn't know what Bridget's problem was. She told him that it took more that a minute's stimulation for her to be orgasmic and he wanted to oblige, but he couldn't keep himself from ejaculating before he wanted to come.

> Sandy was so excited by his date that he came as soon as she touched his penis through his clothes. Her disappointment was obvious and he was extremely reluctant to try again with anyone.

> Tony never thought much about what his partner wanted. He saw "getting off" as a job to be done and the quicker, the better. He appeared for treatment only because his wife refused to have sex with him unless he did.

Historically, the conditions of hurry-up sex alone or in early partner experiences may have sensitized the system to fast-track orgasm. The man who ejaculates prematurely has not learned where his point of inevitability is or how to engage in sexually stimulating activity below that point of arousal until he wants to have the orgasm. Ejaculation is a threshold phenomenon. When the penis is stimulated to that point, ejaculation occurs. The treatment goal is obvious; stay below the threshold.

Many men who come quickly try to distract themselves in hopes of lasting longer: "If I think about something else, then

I'll slow down." They try to remember old songs or Mickey Mantle's batting averages, recite Masonic rituals, work out chess moves, make up the grocery list, or do anything else to keep from thinking about what they are doing. Wrong. First, it feels better for a man to be there with himself and his partner. Second, it is essential that he be aware of how aroused he is in order that he not go over the threshold, the point of inevitability or point of ejaculatory premonition (sounds rather mystical), until he wants to do so.

Originally, therapists suggested a trial and error approach to stopping before it was too late to stop. In 1956, Dr. James Semans described the "stop-start" technique: a few strokes or thrusts, stop until the level of arousal goes down, start stroking again, stop, start, and so on, all to keep the stimulation going—but not intensely enough to trigger an ejaculation.[9] Masters and Johnson refined the concept by adding the "squeeze technique." While stopped, the man or his partner would squeeze the penis for several seconds until the erection was partially lost and the urgency to ejaculate had passed.[10] This sounds like a game of brinksmanship, and it was. Although it would have been framed by the sex therapist as a learning experience so that a man would realize when he had gone too far and not go as far the next time, it would still be frustrating and guess work. Debate among therapists raged (or simmered a little, at least) about where to squeeze, how long to squeeze, and the best position in which to do all this. The consensus was anywhere along the shaft of the penis for twenty to thirty seconds with the woman in the superior position. Those who figured out the instructions got results. Many did.

A real advance in treatment came with psychiatrist Helen Singer Kaplan's 1990 book about premature ejaculation. She suggested what now seems obvious, to build an internal ten-point scale from zero for no arousal to ten for ejaculatory inevitability and to learn to identify and monitor the level of arousal.[11] For example, a man could stop the stimulation at level seven or eight and start again when it dropped to three or four and then gradually learn to stay longer just below the brink. This has been a simple but completely reasonable solution to the dilemma of how to "stop just before it's too late to stop." The man also needs to practice more frequently as this makes individual attempts less stimulating and reverses the usual pattern of frustration leading to fewer and fewer tries. This approach encourages a man to pay more attention to what is going on in his own body, to be aware of his feelings of arousal, and to learn how to be in control of himself. The information that he gains from paying attention to his feelings allows him to become more competent and confident in this area. Graham and Bridget were highly motivated and practiced several times a week. It took only a few weeks for Graham to last several minutes and for Bridget to be reliably orgasmic.

So far, we have discussed only "stimulation" to various levels of arousal, but not technique itself. Some men who were conditioned to masturbate quickly (remember the little brother pounding on the bathroom door or the worry that mother would come in if the bed continued to squeak?) still come quickly under all conditions. It is logical therefore, for those men to start the relearning process by practicing the "stay below the threshold" technique during masturbation. Changing the venue from the toilet or the squeaky bed and modifying the grip or the speed would help to interrupt the old pattern. One could move from dry rubbing to more stimulating lubricated masturbation and even add different fantasies in order to vary the level of arousal.

Even if a man lasts for hours with masturbation but comes quickly during intercourse because of a hurry-up history (the back seat of a car in lovers' lane or the living room couch with her parents upstairs) it is helpful to learn about the sensation of threshold (and most premature ejaculators do not) by masturbating. Sandy was happy to start with this exercise and was able to confidently maintain an erection for several minutes before ejaculating. Once the technique of staying below the point of inevitability has been mastered, a man logically goes on to vaginal penetration (perhaps a significant problem in itself) and continues to apply the same behavioral principle. He thrusts to higher levels of arousal, stops until the level drops, proceeds with thrusting, and so on, so that he builds up to several minutes of erection and containment without ejaculation. Luckily for Sandy, he met a woman who understood the problem and sympathetically and patiently helped him to be successful.

A word about penetration. It is often the exciting sensation of containment of the penis by the vagina that itself triggers the ejaculation. If this is a specific problem, then an additional step is required. This is called "stuffing" or putting a flaccid, nonerect penis into the vagina and then doing nothing except logging time inside without ejaculating. Here a man is teaching his penis to be inside without coming, or, in psychological terms, to decondition the stimulus of containment from the response of ejaculation. A man could logically practice this while learning the masturbation exercise so that the first penetration by an erect penis could be at a lower point on the scale toward ejaculation and more control would be possible. No one is perfect, and should response speed up in the future, as it commonly does, then the man must return to a focus on the level of arousal and slow down the whole process again.

Tony was so angry at his wife for withholding sex that he started seeing another woman who didn't complain about quickies. His wife left him. Therapy cannot resolve every conflict.

This discussion is not meant to be an exhaustive and exhausting exposition of all aspects of sex therapy. Rather it points up the role that masturbation plays in the treatment of sexual problems. It is useful in modifying potentially inappropriate fantasy by learning to pair the pleasure of orgasm with a more "appropriate" thought. It is helpful in building previously low levels of desire by associating pleasure with erotic thoughts. A woman can learn the most effective way to produce an orgasm. A man can learn to reshape badly learned ejaculatory behavior with masturbatory practice in defining threshold and learning to stay below it. He can enjoy masturbatory success in reducing performance anxiety prior to working with a partner. Masturbation is therapeutic.

NOTES

1. William Masters and Virginia Johnson, *Human Sexual Inadequacy* (Boston: Little, Brown & Co., 1970).

2. Fred Beliveau and Lin Richler, *Understanding Human Sexual Inadequacy* (Boston: Little, Brown & Co., 1970).

3. Jack Annon, *The Behavioral Treatment of Sexual Problems: Brief Therapy* (Honolulu: Enabling Systems, 1976).

4. American Association of Sex Educators, Counselors, and Therapists, Suite 2-A, 103 A Avenue South, Mount Vernon, IA 52314, online at www.aasect.org.

5. Gene Abel, Judith Becker, and Linda Skinner, "Behavioral Approaches to Treatment of the Violent Sex Offender," in *Clinical Treatment of the Violent Person*, ed. Loren Roth (Rockville, Md.: National Institute of Mental Health, 1985).

6. Edward Rowan, Judith Rowan, and Pamela Langlier, "Women who Molest Children," *Bulletin of the American Academy of Psychiatry and the Law* 18 (1990): 79–83.

7. Bernie Zilbergeld, *The New Male Sexuality* (New York: Bantam, 1992).

8. Sandra Leiblum and Raymond Rosen, ed., *Principles and Practice of Sex Therapy* (New York: Guilford, 1984), p. 89.

9. James Semans, "Premature Ejaculation: A New Approach," *Southern Medical Journal* 49 (1956): 353–57.

10. Masters and Johnson, *Human Sexual Inadequacy*, p. 102.

11. Helen Singer Kaplan, *Premature Ejaculation* (New York: Brunner/Mazel, 1990).

Chapter Twelve

■

Getting in Touch

■

A series of exercises can help men and women redis-cover their sensual selves and go beyond mechanical self-pleasuring and friction to self-awareness, unlimited sensual pleasure, and, ultimately, integration of sensuality into their relationships. The paths are the same but the journey is different for men and women. Men, in general, need to slow down and learn to enjoy the trip rather than achieve the goal. They already know how to jump the line and race to the end. Women, in general, need to explore the path to an as yet unachieved goal. Both can experience the pleasure of the journey to learn about themselves and to try different techniques and side paths in pursuit of that most personal of all pleasures, the uninhibited orgasm.

A note to men: read the instructions before proceeding. There is prep work to be done before firing up the grill, a manual to read before tinkering with the engine, and plan-ning to be considered before reaching for the tool.

The first exercise is an inventory of sexual attitudes, feel-ings, and experiences. From the beginning, it is important to be attuned to the genital self. The second exercise is the discovery of the best conditions for a good sensual experience and the optimal setting for self-pleasuring. After that, we get to the genitals. The sensation of orgasm and ejaculation may release a flood of feelings that require attention as well as integration into relationships.

This is a guidebook for a journey beyond friction, a journey to change the fundamental ways we think about masturbation. It is not a substitute but an alternative, not genital focus but whole-body experience, not a physical phenomenon but a spiritual one.

This journey is not a new idea, just a different tour. Several books already include suggested exercises for getting in touch with inner feelings, but for many different reasons.[1] Women have taken the journey as part of a program to become orgasmic. For men it is not an exercise in becoming orgasmic, but one to get in touch with sexual feelings and to refocus masturbatory behavior. Women naturally think in terms of talking to friends or working in groups. Men don't operate that way. As you do the exercises, you may see the value of sharing experiences and feelings. In many ways, a training group would be ideal for this, but a trusted friend or therapist will do, or feelings can stay inside just as they always have.

The exercises are divided into four groups. Everything is optional. The sequence is logical and builds upon what has gone before, but you may want to skip some pieces or modify them to suit your needs. If you are stuck, then go back and try to understand what old tape is playing in your mind and blocking your progress. Relax, and have a good trip.

TAKING AN INVENTORY

This phrase is borrowed from our friends recovering from addictions. The first step is to take an inventory of your sex life: your attitudes, feelings, and experiences. It could also be called a sex history. Each of us needs a clear picture of our own history and the experiences that shaped the way we are today. This inventory is put in question form. Answer the questions in your own mind or get a pad and write down the answers. You might find that notes will be helpful later in the process.

Names

What did you first call "it," your penis or vagina?

Where did you get that label?

As you grew older, did you use other words?

Did it ever have a name?

Thinking back, were there implications of words that were assertive and powerful (pistol), diminutive (dink), babyish (pee-pee), shameful (down there), negative (slash), or cute (muffin)?

Did the words reflect how you felt or how others felt about it at the time?

Do they still?

"Facts"

What were the "facts" about genitals, sex, and masturbation as you first heard them?

Were family members the sources of information and/or role models?

Who, if anyone, told you the "facts of life?"

What did you learn from the "experts" you really respected—the other kids?

Did you have something formally called "sex education"? Was it helpful?

Was there any adult who could and would answer your questions?

Who did you talk to?

Did you learn anything from a medical source, such as a doctor, film, or book?

Consider the above communications in terms of message and metamessage (the nonverbal cues about what is being said). Were there implications such as acceptance, interest, concern, negativity, or revulsion?

Do any of these "factual" messages still have a place in your thinking or feeling?

Guilt

Were you brought up in a formal practice of religion?

What was the religious attitude toward masturbation and other expressions of sexuality?

If not through religious instruction, were shame or guilt conveyed in some other way?

Was there a way to deal with shame and guilt, such as confession?

Is this how you still feel about masturbation and other expressions of sexuality?

If you consider yourself religious now, how does that impact on your views of masturbation and other expressions of sexuality?

First time

Can you remember your first masturbatory experience? Recall it in terms of age, circumstances, and feelings, as well as if self-discovered, observed, or taught.

What did you call it?

Adolescence

What was your pattern of masturbation in terms of frequency, techniques, and favorite fantasies (scripted and unscripted)?

If you stopped, why?

Did you ever have the experience of sharing with others (e.g., a circle jerk)?

Did you ever do or were you ever done by another person? How did it feel?

Adulthood

Has the masturbatory pattern changed?

If you stopped, why?

Does having a partner make a difference?

Does your partner know? Are you sure?

Do you ever talk about the experience or masturbate with a partner or anyone else?

Arousal

Are there people and/or situations which you label as "turn-ons"?

Ditto for "turn-offs"?

Is there a pattern for either?

What are your favorite fantasies? How do they relate to the above?

Lists

Make a list of all the negative things you believe about masturbation.

Make a list of all the positive things. (Don't be surprised if it is shorter.)

Write down three positive statements about masturbation, affirmations that you could really believe.

Relationship

Without peeking, draw a picture of your genitals.

Consider your likes and dislikes, such as circumcised or not, shape, length, girth, scrotum and balls, hair pattern, color, size and shape of lips.

Write a letter to you from your genitals. How would it be addressed?

Dear_____

Some of the really lousy things you've done to me are. . .
Some of the really nice things are. . .
What I would really like you to do for me is. . .

What would you like to tell it about the same topics?

Could you two work out your differences cooperatively?

Physical inventory

Stand in front of a mirror and look at your whole body.

What do you like and what do you dislike?

Now sit down comfortably on a bed or on the floor with pillows behind your back.

Arrange a make-up mirror and bright light and spread your legs. Really look at that cock or cunt. Admire it from all angles. Women, open the lips and identify the clitoris and the hood that covers it.

How accurate was the picture that you drew?

Talk

By now, a lot of conflicting feelings may have come to the surface. You might try talking to yourself about these feelings as if you were your best friend or someone you respected.

What advice would you give to a friend who was having these conflicting feelings?

Perhaps you could put yourself in the role of a prosecuting attorney and then a defense attorney in presenting your case to a jury of sympathetic peers.

What would you say? What are the key points?

Where is the injustice, the injury, or the crime?

Is there fault here, and where does it lie?

Put yourself into the drama of it all. If you cannot work this through at the level of personal feelings, consider doing it with a friend or therapist.

GETTING IN TOUCH

The next stage of the exercise focuses on the body, not on the genitals. First, consider your conditions for relaxation and sensuality, and remember that conditions for good sex apply to masturbation as well. For starters, avoid situations that would lead to guilt, shame, or "getting caught." This is a selfish exercise to discover what feels good for you. Find a comfortable place without interruption (e.g., phone) or distraction (e.g., television.) Music could be positive or negative and may be part of the discovery process, so think about what it is that you put into this sensual pathway. Avoid mind-altering substances. Consider a warm bath and then go whole hog and use bubble bath or lotion. In the bath, bed, or other comfortable spot, rub your hands over your whole body, but not your genitals. Use a lotion or oil to enhance the sensation. What are your erogenous zones (e.g., ears, lips, neck, armpits, nipples, thighs, hands, feet)? As you massage yourself, make a conscious note of what feels good and make positive statements to yourself that it is all right to relax, experience self-pleasure, and feel good. For the jocks, this massage is not to work out muscle tightness, but to soothe and relax.

Reconsider your conditions for good sex in view of your experiences so far:

- What are the best times and places for a sensual experience?
- What is the best mindset?
- Can you counter negative thoughts with positive ones? Are your "affirmations" effective? Change them is they are not.
- Can you let yourself drift into fantasy? If one fantasy doesn't work, then try another.
- Go back to the mirror and look again. Any changes in your perception of yourself?

In preparation for the next phase, it is helpful to get in training and to build up the appropriate muscles. These are the pelvic muscles that spasm during orgasm. They can be identified as the ones that are tightened when trying to hold off urinating or defecating while running to the bathroom. The exercises are named after Dr. Alfred Kegel, who first described them in 1949 for women with postpartum incontinence. After exercising, these women and others reported that their sex lives were better for having stronger pelvic muscles and a better appreciation of the sexual response.[2]

To be sure that you have identified the right muscles, let your urine flow and then try to cut it off. The muscles that you use to cut off the flow are the ones you'll use for the Kegel exercises. Start by simply tightening the muscles quickly fifteen times, twice a day. Initially, the abdominal and thigh muscles may go along, but focus only on the pelvic. Once the muscles are isolated, build up to seventy-five contractions, twice a day. Then try a series of "long" Kegels where the contraction is held for a few seconds before release. One series of short and one series of long per day is recommended. Doing these at a fixed time is helpful. Possible scenarios include while brushing teeth and while traveling back and forth to work. Some sex therapists have suggested doing these exercises when stopped at red lights or when talking on the telephone. Next time you're stopped in traffic, consider what all those other drivers are doing, especially those with the cellular phones. It may take several weeks before results are obvious, but they will be. At the extreme, one man insisted that his pelvic muscles were so toned that he could hang a tee-shirt on his erect penis and wave it back and forth like a flag.

For those of you who do yoga, *ashwini mudra* (contracting the anal sphincter while breathing in) is supposedly superior to Kegels. Check with your guru.

GENITAL PLEASURE

Men

I'll bet you thought that we'd never get to it, and, now that we have, we're going to start by avoiding erections. A soft penis can give pleasure, too. Include your penis in the touching as part of the whole-body pleasuring experience. If "hands-on" stimulation has never been part of your repertoire, it's time to include it now. This is especially so if you would ultimately like to transfer learning to penetration, because a closed hand is a closer approximation to a vagina than a fuzzy blanket is. It is also important to try new things if you are locked into only one narrow technique for being orgasmic. If you do get an erection, then move your hands elsewhere and let the erection subside. Consider how variable touches, pressures, and movements feel and be really aware that a wide range of sensual experience is possible from a "limp dick." On the other hand, don't try to force an erection. If you build up to it, it will come. If you associate wet hands with erections, then try dry first in order to experience soft pleasure. Go on to experience the sensations associated with erection, but avoid ejaculation. Remember that this is a journey, not a race. The focus is on the process, not on the goal. First without and then with lubrication, experiment with different ways of touch, movement, pressure, and speed. Focus on pleasure, not on the erection itself. Practice letting the erection go and then bringing it back. See what effects Kegel exercises might have on intensifying the sensation or on curbing the urge to ejaculate. If orgasm happens, it happens. Consider what you might do to change the pattern and to prolong your exploration next time.

At this point in the journey, the paths diverge. Some may say, "That's nice, but it's time for an orgasm" and be done. Others might spend some time on this plane (not really a plateau) and meditate on the experience. Some with therapeutic goals in mind may need to consider scales of arousal and practice stopping in order to delay ejaculation, while others may be building confidence in erections that have previously been unreliable. Still others may have a special investment in brinksmanship and in recognition of the point of inevitability. Teachers of Tantric yoga counsel stopping the stimulation one stroke before coming and letting the sexual energy rise and open the chakras. Their premise that orgasm would deplete energy will not be debated here. William Hartman believed that "any man can" become "multiorgasmic" by stopping prior to ejaculation and experiencing the psychic (limbic) sensation of orgasm without having the actual ejaculation.[3] Without ejaculation, there is no "refractory period" and the orgasmic sensation can be prolonged.

Time is not a big issue at this stage, as long as it's enough. Less than fifteen minutes is probably insufficient for relearning bad habits. There is no "too long" as far as pleasure is concerned.

Ejaculation is not the goal of the exercises, but if it happens, the experience should be a good one. Prepare for this possibility in advance. Nothing detracts from a good orgasm like running to the bathroom for a handful of tissues. Let fly and enjoy it or have something close by for mopping up. Experiment with technical variations during the ejaculation itself. Consider some of the enhancing techniques such as gently squeezing the testicles or stimulating the anus. Ejaculate as lubricant for further stimulation is a possibility but this may be too intense for some. It is also important to be able to let go. That often includes giving voice to pleasure. If you feel like shouting, why not?

Women

Now that you're comfortable touching and caressing your body, include the clitoris and vaginal area in your exploration. Don't try to apply sustained stimulation—keep moving on to other sensuous sites. By now there will probably be sufficient vaginal lubrication to keep the touch comfortable, but supplement with a water-soluble lubricant if necessary. Once you sense the tension building, back off and let it build again. Orgasms happen when the threshold is reached. Orgasms provide a wide range of experience and if you've never had one, here are some things to look for: a peak of intense feeling that rapidly fades, a vaginal contraction at that peak of intensity, a sudden sense of physical and emotional release.

If your clitoris is too sensitive for direct stimulation, try touching the clitoral hood, pressing the vaginal lips together, or cupping the entire area. A vibrator over layers of cloth may feel better.

Now, don't get discouraged if there is no peak experience. This process may take several sessions. Be sure you are allowing enough time and avoiding potential distraction. Don't schedule your pleasure ten minutes before the kids are due home from school or while you're waiting for an important phone call. Self-pleasuring feels better when you feel good about yourself. If it's been a really bad day, shrug it off and try again another time. You might also consider role-playing an orgasm. This is really a rehearsal of letting go, so roll around, yell, and act silly. A real orgasm will be no worse.

If you have a sense that you're "almost there" add Kegel exercises or bodily tension such as clenched fists or shoulders. Hold your breath. If you are still unsuccessful, try a vibrator. Again, there are many individual variations in response. One woman who had a root canal done without anesthesia had a very high threshold for orgasm as well; she had to use a vibrator for a long time before being successful.

Experiment with different positions, such as on your back, side, or belly with knees drawn up or legs straight. Vary the technique and use different pressures or speeds. Try different strokes, different vibrators, or fingers or dildo in the vagina to feel the muscles contract with orgasm.

Once you've been successful, you have a special capacity that most men lack: multiple orgasm. You can keep going and going and going until you are totally satisfied, exhausted, or both.

AFTER

Women have always treasured the postorgasmic state for its intense reaffirmation of the relationship. Men have stereotypically rolled over and fallen asleep. It really is okay to be open to emotion and to get in touch with the feelings that are released by orgasm. Some people may feel relief, elation, physical warmth, loneliness, abandonment, or oneness with the universe. If you're with someone, it's nice to share. It's also important to realize that change is always difficult and somehow stressful in itself. Even when they try not to, people have a terrible habit of going back to old patterns. If that happens, don't be discouraged. Go back to a step in the series of exercises where you can be successful and do it again. It will probably be a shorter trip the next time and you will have learned a valuable lesson about what blocked your success.

NOTES

1. Three generally available books that contain this approach are: *Becoming Orgasmic: A Sexual Growth Program for Women* by Julia Heiman and Joseph LoPiccolo (Englewood Cliffs, N. J.: Prentice-Hall, 1984); *For Yourself: The Fulfillment of Female Sexuality* by Lonnie Barbach (New York: Doubleday, 1975); and *The New Male Sexuality* by Bernie Zilbergeld (New York: Bantam, 1992).

2. Alfred Kegel, "Sexual Functions of the Pubococcygeous Muscle," *Western Journal of Surgery* 60 (1952): 521–24.

3. William Hartman and Marilyn Fithian, *Any Man Can* (New York: St. Martin's Press, 1984).

Chapter Thirteen

■

Beyond Friction

■

As we've seen, masturbation is a normal part of the life cycle from in utero development to old age. The personal values assigned to it have changed over time in accordance with cultural practice. This is the social constructionist perspective.

As a basic biological function, male masturbation enhances sperm vigor for "sperm wars" and is consistent with Darwinian principles. It occurs in addition to and not as a substitute for procreation. It is inherently pleasurable and subject to positive reinforcement as a result. Masturbation also serves a rehearsal function, especially after the opposable thumb, abstraction, and fantasy enter the evolutionary picture with primates. Masturbation is clearly normal and natural in animals unencumbered by "moral" values. Anthropologists have found masturbation in every culture on earth for which there is information.

In ancient tribes or primitive societies, procreation was the primary goal of sexuality because larger numbers of people were required for survival. Population losses due to war, famine, and disease had to be replaced. Life was hard and denial of physical pleasure to the body in this life was justified by a glorification of the soul in another dimension. Institutionalized religion established the cultural value that sex was for procreation and not for pleasure. In this view, birth control and masturbation served no procreative function and were therefore "unnatural." This was the social construct of masturbation as "sin."

Medicine has historically been intertwined with religion, and the earliest medical views about sexuality supported the "natural" primacy of procreation. Throughout the centuries, faith has worked wonders and many ills have responded to the healing powers of medicine; however, there has always been a tendency to blame the victim when the doctor or the priest could not effect a cure. Over time physical diseases, mental illnesses, and moral shortcomings as consequences of the "unnatural act" have, in turn, dominated the medicocultural construct of masturbation as "sickness." Ultimately, acceptance of the germ theory in the late nineteenth century eliminated the physical degeneration hypothesis, discovery of hormones in the early twentieth eliminated the view of semen as the "vital essence," and psychodynamic formulations in the twentieth eliminated the concepts of masturbatory insanity, neurasthenia, and moral degeneracy.

The most antisexual period of our history was supposed to have been the Victorian age. The dominant event of the era was the expansion of the British Empire, and such expansion required both capitalism and military power. The work imperative required less pleasure and more productivity without wasting or spending sexual capital. Procreation again was primary. The philosopher Michel Foucault has argued persuasively that the Victorian age "repressed" sexuality in a social construct of "silence" only in a political sense. There was extensive discourse about sex in other areas, such as the titillation of the confessional and the warnings of medical practice. This culturally approved version of sexuality was economically useful and politically conservative.[1] Masturbation only served to encourage individuals to withdraw from the larger collective enterprise. Suppression brought us a range of inventions to keep children from touching themselves, and it triggered the introduction of such diverse institutions for clean living as Kellogg's corn flakes, Graham's crackers, and Baden-Powell's Boy Scouts. This construct persisted well into the twentieth century.

Major changes occurred after World War II. Mind-numbing events such as the Holocaust and the use of nuclear weapons caused people to reconsider the notion that society, as it existed, could ever be enlightened. If one cannot count on society, then one can count only on oneself. The cultural trend has moved to the primacy of the individual and the psychology of self-actualization. To quote the motto of the State University of New York, "Let each become all that he is capable of being." "Turn on, tune in, and drop out" and the "Me generation" became the extremes of this perspective.

Contemporary social construction is a narrative of the self. Sexual fulfillment is part of self-fulfillment. Masturbation now fits positively into that process. Pleasurable in itself, it is also a rehearsal process as well as part of healing. Sex therapy, as we understand it, depends on rehearsing and reshaping dysfunctional behavior through masturbation. Given the risks of sexually transmitted diseases, masturbation has become the ultimate form of safe sex. Environmental concern now supports population control instead of unrestricted procreation.

For many men, midlife (or earlier) is a time to review our multiple sources of sex-negativity and the masculine construct that sexuality is synonymous with mastery and control. One potential midlife transition is to chart a new course of self-discovery and self-determination. Reflection on successes and failures in life may actually start us looking at feelings and relationships. The new male psychology suggests that we look within to recapture that very early sense of wonder in our bodies and in our experience of the world. Women may finally be able to move beyond being passive receptacles and experience the sexual energy of pure pleasure.

This journey beyond friction is lifelong and the process of self-discovery never ends. Our bodies change, as does the world around us. We now should have the tools with which to look at the process. Bodily pleasure and sensuality are basic elements of life, despite what the socialization process has done to them. By attending to internal messages, we no longer have to rely on external control and authority figures to tell us what is right. We can challenge the notion that pleasure is inherently evil and has to be controlled. We can be trusted to make the right decisions for ourselves. If enough of us subscribe to this cause, then we can ultimately change the social contract.

Those familiar with the work of Joseph Campbell will find parallels here. Campbell studied the myths and legends of many civilizations and found a universal pattern or monomyth—the hero's journey.[2] The hero's journey begins with the decision to undertake an adventure, a vision quest, or a rite of passage in order to leave the present world of life patterns, attachments, and attitudes and to search for what is missing.

Dark forces attempt to block passage as the hero journeys through a world of unfamiliar yet strangely intimate experiences. He clarifies the problems and eradicates them, sometimes with the help of a mentor. Finally he undergoes a supreme ordeal to gain his reward, a power, a special favor, or a personal enlightenment. There he finds not a discovery, but a rediscovery of parts of himself which expand power and renew life.

The hero could then retreat from the world into that state of personal enlightenment or he could return to regenerate society with that power. He brings life to the world by finding it in himself, becoming truly alive, "following his bliss," and letting that life force flow into the body of the world.

The journey proposed here is like that. The decision to move beyond the stereotypes of sex and masturbation as elements of pleasureless power and control or passive receptivity is blocked by the dark forces of guilt and shame and by the ogres of sin, sickness, and silence. We brush against the strange feelings of wonder, pleasure, and sensuality and ultimately break through to a sense of enlightenment and personal freedom. We return from the journey to share that experience of intimacy.

The masturbation myth has been told many times, but the moral has been corrupted by social constructs. Onan was a hero. He defied the existing rules for ejaculation but was killed by an angry father. A different version of Genesis might have seen him as a champion of freedom, a self-actualized man who thought for himself, a man who believed that a relationship with a woman implied more than impregnation, a man who wanted his children to identify him as their father, and a man who taught others to do the right thing. He might have been resurrected a hero. Unfortunately for him, that myth was reserved for someone else.

Wilhelm Stekel was a hero. He described the person who masturbated as "autotheos," his own god.[3] He clearly recognized the power in personal freedom and enlightenment but was unable to bring the message back from the journey because it died for lack of translation.

Robert Bly and Sam Keen describe hero's journeys. Bly focuses on the mentor who helps along the way and Keen on the inner journey to enlightenment, but both miss the importance of masturbation.[4] Suppression of masturbation and focus on procreation are key in our rite of passage from adolescence to adulthood. The stereotypes have been maintained, but we now have an opportunity to make sense out of the prohibition and suppression and to see it for the ancient and no longer necessary rite that it is. We have a choice to transition to the rules of our fathers or to confront them and change them.

It was Carl Jung who pointed out that the real task of midlife is for the hero to give way to the anima.[5] The "anima" is the "eros," or female principle of relatedness, that a man must develop in order to better connect to himself and his fellow humans. This is analogous to the "animus," the "logos" or male principle of discrimination, judgment, and insight, that women must develop so that they, too, become whole. From Jung's perspective, heroism is a young person's game. The task of the second half of life is to integrate heroism and relatedness and to transmit that cultural heritage to the next generation. We now have the opportunity to mentor budding heroes and to help these younger people (including our own children) on their journey. We can guide them in taming the dark forces of guilt and shame and the ogres of sin, sickness, and silence who lurk on the road to self-discovery.

Call it anima, generativity, or mentoring. It's a different way to be in the world: accepting sensual pleasure in our bodies, valuing relatedness, integrating experiences—including painful ones—into our lives, and guiding others along the same path.

We've met Irv before, and I think it is worthwhile to repeat his thoughts: "I really like doing myself. I take it very slowly and use massage oil to rub all over my cock. I like to tease myself right up to the edge and then stop. After a couple of those, I have a powerful come that make me want to yell, it feels so good. I'm high for hours." By now it should be clear how a "grown man" could think this way. For Irv, masturbation is a positive experience, not a "poor substitute" for "real sex" with a partner. Like most of us, Irv has a partner, too. Ann knows that he takes that special time for himself and that she has the same opportunity. She believes that it makes each of them more sensitive and their relationship better. They feel good about masturbation and try to share that positive attitude with their children. Those kids represent the best hope for a change in attitudes in the next millennium.

Unfortunately, acceptance of masturbation is not the same as an affirmation of it. We must go beyond simply saying "it's normal" and promote solo sex as a positive activity that every man, woman, and child should be doing. We should be promoting joy, pride, and satisfaction in masturbation. When we heighten sexual pleasure, mobilize sexual energy, and own our own sexuality, it changes the way we relate to others. We don't need them to fulfill us; they don't need us to make them whole. Imagine the changes that could happen in the world if all the positive energy of pure pleasure were channeled to the common good.

Masturbation is an integral part of life and a potential path to positive sexual expression and discovery. It may become a spiritual quest. The choice to take it is yours.

NOTES

1. Michel Foucault, *The History of Sexuality*, vol. 1: *An Introduction* (New York: Pantheon, 1976).

2. Joseph Campbell, *The Hero With a Thousand Faces* (New York: Bollingen, 1949).

3. Wilhelm Stekel, *Autoeroticism* (London: Liveright, 1950).

4. Robert Bly, *Iron John* (Reading, Mass.: Addison-Wesley, 1990); and Sam Keen, *Fire in the Belly* (New York: Bantam, 1991).

5. Carl Jung, *Aspects of the Masculine* (Princeton: Princeton University Press, 1989).

References

Abel, Gene, Judith Becker, and Linda Skinner. "Behavioral Approaches to the Treatment of the Violent Sex Offender." In *Clinical Treatment of the Violent Person*, edited by Loren Roth. Rockville, Md.: National Institute of Mental Health, 1985.

Alzate, Heli. "Sexual Behavior of Unmarried Colombian University Students: A Follow-up." *Archives of Sexual Behavior* 18 (1989): 239–50.

Ammar, Hamed. *Growing Up in an Egyptian Village: Silwa, Province of Aswan*. London: Routledge & Kegan Paul Ltd., 1954.

American Medical Association. *Human Sexuality*. Chicago: AMA, 1972.

Annon, Jack. *The Behavioral Treatment of Sexual Problems: Brief Therapy*. Honolulu: Enabling Systems, 1976.

Baden-Powell, Robert S. S. *Rovering to Success*. London: Pearson, 1927.

Baker, Robin. *Sperm Wars: The Science of Sex*. New York: Basic Books, 1996.

Barbach, Lonnie. *For Yourself: The Fulfillment of Female Sexuality*. New York: Doubleday, 1975.

———. *Discovering Orgasm Workbook*. Bristol, Penn.: Brunner/ Mazel, 1997.

Bauserman, Robert. "Fantasy in Childhood and Adolescence: An Exploratory Study." Paper presented at the annual meeting of the Society for the Scientific Study of Sexuality, Chicago, 1993.

Belcastro, Phillip. "Sexual Behavior Differences Between Black and White Students." *Journal of Sex Research* 21 (1985): 56–67.

Beliveau, Fred, and Lin Richler. *Understanding Human Sexual Inadequacy*. Boston: Little, Brown & Co., 1970.

Betchen, Stephen. "Male Masturbation as a Vehicle for the Pursuer/Distancer Relationship in Marriage." *Journal of Sex and Marital Therapy* 17 (1991): 269–78.

Blank, Joni. *The Playbook for Men About Sex*. Burlingame, Calif.: Down There Press, 1975.

———. *First Person Sexual*. San Francisco: Down There Press, 1996.

Bly, Robert. *Iron John*. Reading, Mass.: Addison-Wesley, 1990.

Brenner, Charles. *An Elementary Textbook of Psychoanalysis*. Garden City: Doubleday, 1955.

Budge, E. A. Wallis. *The Gods of the Egyptians*. Vol. 1. London: Methuen & Co., 1904.

Bullough, Vern. *Sexual Variance in Society and History*. New York: John Wiley & Sons, 1976.

———. *Science in the Bedroom*. New York: Basic Books, 1994.

Bullough, Vern, and Bonnie Bullough. *Sin, Sickness, and Sanity*. New York: Garland, 1977.

Calderwood, Derek. *About Your Sexuality*. Boston: Unitarian Universalist Association, 1983.

Campbell, Joseph. *The Hero with a Thousand Faces*. New York: Bollingen, 1949.

Catania, Joseph, Lois McDermott, and Lance Pollack. "Questionnaire Response Bias and Face-to-Face Interview Sample Bias in Sexuality Research." *Journal of Sex Research* 22 (1986): 52–72.

Chan, David. "Sex Knowledge, Attitudes, and Experiences of Chinese Medical Students in Hong Kong." *Archives of Sexual Behavior* 19 (1990): 73–94.

Cornog, Martha. "The Circle Game: Social Masturbation for Young and Old(er)." Paper presented at the Midwest Chapter of the Society for the Scientific Study of Sexuality, Madison, Wis., 1999.

Davidson, Kenneth, and Linda Hoffman. "Sexual Fantasies and Sexual Satisfaction: An Empirical Analysis of Erotic Thought." *Journal of Sex Research* 22 (1986): 184–205.

Diamond, Norma. *Kún Shen: A Taiwan Village.* New York: Holt, Reinhart & Winston, 1969.

Dodson, Betty. *Liberating Masturbation.* Self-published, 1974.

———. *Sex for One: The Joy of Self-Loving.* New York: Harmony Books, 1987.

Dube, S. C. *Indian Village.* Ithaca: Cornell University Press, 1955.

Edwards, James. "The Exotic Other: Koro and the Retractile Penis." Paper presented at the Twelfth World Congress on Sexology, Yokohama, Japan, 1995.

Ellis, Albert. *Sex and the Single Male.* New York: Lyle Stuart, 1950.

Ellis, Havelock. *Studies in the Psychology of Sex.* Philadelphia: F. A. Davis, 1900.

Elwin, Verrier. *The Muria and Their Gotul.* Bombay: Oxford University Press, 1947.

Evans-Pritchard, E. E. *Witchcraft Among the A-Zande.* Oxford: Clarendon Press, 1937.

Farrell, Michael, and Stanley Rosenberg. *Men at Midlife.* Dover, Mass.: Auburn House, 1981.

Filas, Francis. *Sex Education in the Family.* Englewood Cliffs, N.J.: Prentice-Hall, 1966.

Firth, Raymond. *We the Tikopia: A Sociological Study of Kinship in Primitive Polynesia.* London: Gage, Allen and Unwin Ltd., 1936.

Fog, Eva, J. Lunde, K. Garde, and G. Larsen. "Sexualverhalten, erfahrungen, wissen und einstellungen Dänischer frauen." In *Praktische Sexual Medizine,* edited by Wolf Eicher. Wiesbaden: Verlag Medical Tribune GmbH, 1987.

Ford, Clellen, and Frank Beach. *Patterns of Sexual Behavior.* New York: Harper and Row, 1951.

Foucault, Michel. *The History of Sexuality,* Vol. 1: *An Introduction.* New York: Pantheon, 1976.

Fox, Thomas. *Sexuality and Catholicism.* New York: George Braziller, 1995.

Francoeur, Robert, ed. *International Encyclopedia of Sexuality.* New York: Continuum, 1997.

Fried, Jacob. "Ideal Norms and Social Control in Tarahumara Society." Ph.D. diss., Yale University, 1951.

Freud, Sigmund. *Three Contributions to the Theory of Sex*. London: Hogarth Press, 1905.

Friday, Nancy. *My Secret Garden: Women's Sexual Fantasies*. New York: Pocket Books, 1973.

———. *Forbidden Flowers: More Women's Sexual Fantasies*. New York: Simon & Schuster, 1975.

———. *Men in Love*. New York: Laurel, 1980.

Gagnon, John. "Attitudes and Responses of Parents to Preadolescent Masturbation." *Archives of Sexual Behavior* 14 (1985): 451–66.

———. "The Explicit and Implicit Use of the Scripting Perspective in Sex Research." *Annual Review of Sex Research* 1 (1990): 1–43.

Garza-Leal, Alberto, and Francisco Landrón. "Autoerotic Asphyxial Death Initially Misinterpreted as Suicide and a Review of the Literature." *Journal of Forensic Sciences* 36 (1991): 1753–59.

Gilligan, Carol. *In a Different Voice*. Cambridge: Harvard University Press, 1982.

Gladwin, Thomas, and Seymour Sarason. *Truk: Man in Paradise*. New York: Wennen-Gren Foundation for Anthropological Research, 1953.

Gold, Steven, and Ruth Gold. "Gender Differences in First Sexual Fantasies." *Journal of Sex Education and Therapy* 17 (1991): 207–16.

Gordon, Sol. *The Teenage Survival Book*. New York: Times Books, 1988.

Gorer, Geoffrey. *Himalayan Village: An Account of the Lepchas of Sikkim*. London: Michael Joseph Ltd., 1938.

Greydanus, Donald, and Barbara Geller. "Masturbation: Historic perspective." *New York State Journal of Medicine* 80 (1980): 1892–96.

Hagmaier, George, and Robert Gleason. *Counselling the Catholic*. New York: Sheed & Ward, 1959.

Hall, Winfield Scott. *From Youth into Manhood*. New York: YMCA Press, 1910.

Hamilton, Eleanor. *Sex With Love*. Boston: Beacon Press, 1978.

Hartman, William, and Marilyn Fithian. *Any Man Can*. New York: St. Martin's Press, 1984.

Hazelwood, Robert, Park Dietz, and Ann Burgess. *Autoerotic Fatalities*. Lexington, Mass.: D. D. Heath, 1983.

Heiman, Julia, and Joseph LoPiccolo. *Becoming Orgasmic: A Sexual Growth Program for Women*. 2d ed. Englewood Cliffs, N.J.: Prentice-Hall, 1984.

Henry, Jules, and Zunia Henry. *Doll Play of Pilaga Indian Children*. New York: Vintage Books, 1974.

Hillman, James. "Towards the Archetypal Model for Masturbation Inhibition." In *Loose Ends*. Dallas: Spring Publications, 1975.

Hite, Shere. *The Hite Report*. New York: Macmillan, 1976.

———. *The Hite Report on Male Sexuality*. New York: Knopf, 1981.

Hollomon, Regina. *Developmental Changes in San Blas*. Ann Arbor, Mich.: University Microfilm International, 1969.

Holmberg, Allen. The Siriono: A Study of the Effect of Hunger Frustration on the Culture of a Semi-Nomadic Bolivian Tribe. Ph.D. diss., Yale University, 1946.

Honigman, John. *Culture and Ethos of Kaska Society*. New Haven: Yale University Press for the Department of Anthropology, 1949.

Horney, Karen. *Feminine Psychology*. New York: W. W. Norton, 1967.

Houpt, Katherine, and Gwendolyn Wollney. "Frequency of Masturbation and Time Budgets of Dairy Bulls Used for Semen Production." *Applied Animal Behaviour Science* 24 (1989): 217–25.

Hulstaert, Gustave. *Marriage Among the Nkundu*. Brussells: Van-Campenhout, 1938.

Hunt, Edward, David Schneider, Nathaniel Kidder, and William Stevens. *The Micronesians of Yap and Their Depopulation*. Washington, D.C:. National Research Council, 1949.

Hunt, Morton. *Sexual Behavior in the 1970s*. Chicago: Playboy Press, 1974.

Jung, Carl. *Aspects of the Masculine*. Princeton: Princeton University Press, 1989.

Junod, Henri. *The Life of a South African Tribe*. London: Macmillan & Co., 1927.

Kaplan, Helen Singer. The New Sex Therapy. New York: Brunner/Mazel, 1974.

———. *Disorders of Sexual Desire*. New York: Brunner/Mazel, 1979.

———. *Premature Ejaculation.* New York: Brunner/Mazel, 1990.

Keen, Sam. *Fire in the Belly.* New York: Bantam, 1991.

Kenyatta, Jomo. *Facing Mount Kenya.* London: Secker & Warburg, 1953.

Kimball, Spencer. *The Miracle of Forgiveness.* Salt Lake City: Bookcraft, 1969.

Kinsey, Alfred, Wardell Pomeroy, and Clyde Martin. *Sexual Behavior in the Human Male.* Philadelphia: W. B. Saunders, 1948.

Kinsey, Alfred, Wardell Pomeroy, Clyde Martin, and Paul Gebhard. *Sexual Behavior in the Human Female.* Philadelphia: W. B. Saunders, 1953.

Krafft-Ebing, Richard von. *Psychopathia Sexualis.* New York: Stein and Day, 1886.

Kuchinsky, Berl. "Pornography and Rape: Theory and Practice?" *International Journal of Law and Psychiatry* 14 (1991): 47–64.

Laing, R. D. *The Self and Others.* London: Tavistock, 1959.

Laumann, Edward, John Gagnon, Robert Michael, and Stuart Michaels. *The Social Organization of Sexuality.* Chicago: University of Chicago Press, 1994.

Leitenberg, Harold, Mark Detzer, and Debra Srebnick. "Gender Differences in Masturbation and the Relation of Masturbatory Experience in Preadolescence and/or Early Adolescence to Sexual Behavior and Sexual Adjustment in Young Adulthood." *Archives of Sexual Behavior* 22 (1993): 87–98.

Levins, Hoag. *American Sex Machines.* Holbrook, Mass.: Adams Media Corp., 1996.

Linton, Ralph. "Marquesan Culture." In *The Individual and His Society: The Psychodynamics of Primitive Social Organization,* edited by Abram Kardiner. New York: Columbia University Press, 1939.

Litton, Harold. *Solo Sex: Advanced Techniques.* 2d ed. Mobile, Ala.: Factor Press, 1992.

———. *More Joy . . . An Advanced Guide to Solo Sex.* Mobile, Ala.: Factor Press, 1996.

Lukianowicz, N. "Imaginary Sexual Partners and Visual Masturbatory Fantasies." *Archives of General Psychiatry* 3 (1960): 429–49.

MacNeill, John, and Helen Ganner. *Medieval Handbooks of Penance.* New York: Octagon, 1965.

Malinowski, Bronislaw. *The Sexual Life of Savages in Northwestern Melanesia*. New York: Horace Liveright, 1929.

Margulis, Lynn, and Dorion Sagan. *Origins of Sex*. New Haven: Yale University Press, 1986.

Masters, R. E. L. *Sexual Self-Stimulation*. Los Angeles: Sherbourne Press, 1967.

Masters, William, and Virginia Johnson. *Human Sexual Response*. Boston: Little, Brown & Co., 1966.

———. *Human Sexual Inadequacy*. Boston: Little, Brown & Co., 1970.

Maudsley, Henry. *Pathology of the Mind*. New York: D. Appleton & Co., 1880.

May, Robert. *Sex and Fantasy*. New York: W. W. Norton, 1980.

McDonnell, S. M., et al. "Imipramine-Induced Erection, Masturbation, and Ejaculation in Male Horses." *Pharmacology, Biochemistry, & Behavior* 27(1987): 187–91.

McWhirter, David, and Andrew Mattison. *The Male Couple: How Relationships Develop*. Englewood Cliffs, N.J.: Prentice-Hall, 1984.

Mead, Margaret. *Coming of Age in Samoa*. New York: Morris Quill, 1928.

———. *Growing Up in New Guinea*. New York: Morris Quill, 1930.

Meyer, Hans. *Die Barundi*. Leipzig: O H Spamer, 1916.

Money, John. *The Destroying Angel*. Amherst, N.Y.: Prometheus Books, 1985.

Money, John, Gordon Wainwright, and David Hinsburger. *The Breathless Orgasm*. Amherst, N.Y.: Prometheus Books, 1991.

Morin, Jack. *Men Loving Themselves*. Burlingame, Calif.: Down There Press, 1988.

Morris, John. *Living with Lepchas: A Book About the Sikkim Himalayas*. London: Wm. Heinemann Ltd., 1938.

Mosher, Don. "Three Dimensions of Depth of Involvement in Human Sexual Response." *Journal of Sex Research* 16 (1980): 1–42.

Murray, William. *Rowanduz: A Kurdish Administrative and Mercantile Center*. Ph.D. diss., University of Michigan, 1953.

Nagoa, K. Poster presentation at the Twelfth World Congress on Sexology, Yokohama, Japan, 1995.

Office of the General Assembly of the Presbyterian Church (U.S.A.). *Decisions of the 203rd General Assembly on Sexuality.* Louisville, Ky., 1991.

Peter, Prince of Greece. *A Study of Polyandry.* The Hague: Monton & Co., 1963.

Pongthai, S. Poster presentation at the Twelfth World Congress on Sexology, Yokohama, Japan, 1995.

Rahner, Karl, ed. *Sacramentum Mundi.* New York: Herder & Herder, 1970.

Ranke-Heinemann, Uta. *Eunuchs for the Kingdom of Heaven: Women, Sexuality, and the Catholic Church.* New York: Penguin, 1990.

Reichel-Dormatoff, Gerado. *The Kogi: A Tribe of the Sierra Nevada de Santa Marta.* Bogota: El Instituto Ethnologico Nacional, 1951.

Reinisch, June. *The Kinsey Institute New Report on Sex.* New York: St. Martin's Press, 1990.

Roheim, Geza. *The Eternal Ones of the Dream.* New York: International Universities Press, 1945.

Rosenthal, Michael. *The Character Factory.* New York: Pantheon, 1986.

Rowan, Edward. "Masturbation According to the *Boy Scout Handbook.*" *Journal of Sex Education and Therapy* 15 (1989): 77–81.

Rowan, Edward, Judith Rowan, and Pamela Langlier. "Women Who Molest Children." *Bulletin of the American Academy of Psychiatry and the Law* 18 (1990): 79–83.

Rush, Benjamin. *Medical Inquiries and Observations upon the Diseases of the Mind.* Philadelphia: Griggs & Elliot, 1812.

Shirokogoroff, S. M. *Social Organization of the Manchus.* Shanghai: Royal Asiatic Society, 1924.

Simon, William. "Deviance as History: The Failure of Perversion." *Archives of Sexual Behavior* 23 (1994): 1–21.

Stekel, Wilhelm. *Autoeroticism.* London: Liveright, 1950.

Stoller, Robert. *Sexual Excitement: Dynamics of Erotic Life.* New York: Pantheon, 1979.

Strassberg, Donald, and Lisa Lockerd. "Force in Women's Sexual Fantasies." *Archives of Sexual Behavior* 27(1998): 403–14.

Suggs, Robert. *Marquesas Sexual Behavior.* Yale University, unpublished paper. 1963.

Tannen, Deborah. *That's Not What I Meant*. New York: Ballantine, 1986.

———. *You Just Don't Understand*. New York: Ballantine, 1990.

Tissot, Samuel A. D. *A Treatise on the Diseases Produced by Onanism*. New York: Collins & Hannay, 1832.

Trevett, Reginald. *The Church and Sex*. New York: Hawthorn, 1960.

Tschopik, Harry. "The Aymara of Chuchito, Peru." *Anthropological Papers of the American Museum of Natural History* 44 (1951): 133–308.

Turnbull, Colin. *Wayward Servants: The Two Worlds of the African Pygmies*. Garden City, N.Y.: Natural History Press, 1965.

Walters, Mark. *The Dance of Life: Courtship in the Animal Kingdom*. New York: Arbor House, 1988.

Weinberg, Martin, and Colin Williams. "Black Sexuality: A Test of Two Theories." *Journal of Sex Research* 25 (1988): 197–218.

Wellings, Kaye, Julia Field, Anne Johnson, and Jane Wadsworth. *Sexual Behaviour in Britain*. London: Penguin, 1994.

Winks, Cathy, and Anne Semans. *The New Good Vibrations Guide to Sex*. 2d ed. San Francisco: Cleis Press, 1997.

Woods, Margo. *Masturbation, Tantra, and Self Love*. San Diego: Omphaloskepsis Press, 1981.

Zilbergeld, Bernie. *Male Sexuality*. New York: Bantam, 1978.

———. *The New Male Sexuality*. New York: Bantam, 1992.

Appendix

———————————— ■ ————————————

Websites
for Wankers

———————————— ■ ————————————

My search engine found 737,270 Web sites for "masturbation." These are primarily pornographic sites for jerking off: "Get a hold of yourself, visit the best adult site on the web, and get a load off." For positive, factual information about masturbation as well as humor, questions and answers, personal experiences, and contact lists, try the Sex Education Web Circle at **www.sexuality.org**, which describes itself as "factually accurate and pleasure positive." Included in this group of sites are **www.jackinworld.com** and **www.proaxis.com/~solo/hme.htm**. Jackinworld has a spinoff site, JackinForHer, temporarily located at **www.geocities.com/Wellesley/Atrium/9135**. Solo— Fact and Fantasy in Sexual Satisfaction also has a large section for women, including 122 terms for female masturbation. The Sex Information and Education Council of the United States, or SIECUS, has a site at **www.siecus.org**. Under a search for "masturbation" there are thirty-six situations regarding masturbation with a range of responses and what they mean. **www.allaboutsex.org** has a "Sex for

One, Please" section with questions and answers and personal experiences. It is geared to teens as well as adults. **www.bettydodson.com** is Betty's site and is female masturbation positive and offers three good videos. The Celebrate the Self site is **www.solosex.com** and offers books and videos as well. **www.nyjacks.com** has links to other jerk-off club sites. Happy surfing.